Perfecting Your Faith

Perfecting Your Faith

by
Evangelist Lenard Joe Adkins

Perfecting Your Faith

Copyright © 2015 by Lenard Joe Adkins

ISBN: 978-0692556061

Empyrion Publishing
PO Box 784327
Winter Garden, FL
info@EmpyrionPublishing.com

Printed in the United States of America

Table of Contents

GOD'S WORLD OF FAITH

The blueprints of a magnificent structure rest in the hands of the brilliant architect. At this moment it is only a dream on paper. But soon that paper dream will be turned over to the building contractor who will turn that paper dream into a reality.

Every instruction needed to render success is in that blueprint. The final outcome will not be "chance" or performed by luck. If the building ends in failure it will not be charged to the architect who drew the plans. If that contractor follows all of the instructions contained in that blueprint, success can be predicted with absolute certainty. Worry need not enter into the outcome whatsoever because worry is the result of the lack of knowledge and all knowledge is in that blueprint.

The blueprint is God's Word and the structure that it has set out to build is a holy, dedicated, successful, productive and healthy Christian. What appears to be a superhuman is not really so but a man, an image of God. Everything that this godly image needs to lead such a desired life is found in the master plan, the blueprint, God's Word.

Therefore, prepare yourself to enter the courtroom of the ages to engage in a legal battle with the forces of doubts and fears to discover those things that are legally yours and the rights that you possess through the divine will of Jesus Christ.

No attribute within the Christian realm is as necessary as the possession of faith. Without faith the blood of Jesus is in vain, salvation is in vain and God Almighty is reduced to a fantasy.

Within the lids of the Word lay the answers to every man's need. Within that book we are made to know the mysteries which have been hidden from us by customs and traditions. We learn that there is a God and are made to know that He is not a dictator of the universe, but a kind and loving God who desires to do good things for those who believe in Him. From the Bible we learn just what we really are and what we can be if we want to be. The word "sin" becomes a reality and the word "atonement," a sigh of relief. Hell shines itself before our eyes but hope in a man called Jesus takes the horrible scene away. All of this in the lids of a book called the Bible, and yet without faith it becomes a gigantic book of myths and fairy tales.

How common is the word, "faith." It is observed in the ever growing confidence in today's society, today's governments, today's national defense programs, today's scientists and today's knowledge. But these have been proven over and again to be shifting sand while the rock stands as the only thing that is absolute. But where is faith in today's God?

The lack of power, miracles and divine intervention in today's church cannot be questioned. The answer is well known. This is a faithless generation just as Christ predicted that it would be. But these faithless people have grown out of a faithless, institutional church whose image has not been one to covet by her offspring.

The child need not be as the erring parent and neither does a child of God need to follow the failing footsteps of a dying church. The same miracle working faith of the apostles, the prophets and of Abraham can be ours today if we would learn to perfect and cultivate it by studying the blueprint.

Firstly, understand this one thing: tradition is a slave master. Tradition refers to certain things which have been handed down from one generation to another. These may be ideologies which may not have scriptural foundation but one thing is for certain, they can hinder the Truth from performing its work. What I'm about to say to you is not necessarily what you've been taught all of your life. As a matter of fact this subject of faith has been one of the most misconstrued subjects in the Word of God. Some of the things that I shall reveal to you will be shocking, but you'll suddenly come to the knowledge that these facts were in God's Word all the time.

THE KNOWLEDGE OF FAITH

How wonderful it would be to possess an unwavering faith which would always be available to act whenever needed. Why shouldn't this be possible? According to the blueprint, this is possible. But you must first understand just what it is that you are searching for and what this thing called faith really is.

You must first realize that faith is not in a feeling. What a mistake! Some people believe that they have to work up an emotional faith. When they feel good then they say they can believe, but when the chips are down and their feelings are at low tide, faith is nowhere around. Friend, there wasn't any faith here to begin with…just feelings.

If feelings had anything to do with faith then the three Hebrew boys would have been devoured by the fiery furnace. The feelings of Abraham were not always a mountain-top feeling while he waited for the promised son to be born. If feelings played so much a part in faith, then Paul and Silas would have retired in the Philippian jail.

Many people believe their faith to be as a thermometer which goes up and down and their feelings are the atmospheric conditions which motivates the mercury in that thermometer. This simply is not true.

Secondly, faith is not in experiences. How many times have you heard people say, "If I could see a miracle or a sign, then my faith would be increased?" People want to see something, hear something, feel something, to prompt their faith. In Luke 16, Jesus declared that if men refused to believe the words of God through Moses and the prophets, they wouldn't believe any stronger even if they saw one raised from the dead. But then, you can always hear those who will quote Mark 16:20 to prove that signs and wonders are for the purpose of building people's faith. But this isn't true. The Bible says in this verse, "They went forth and preached everywhere, the Lord working with them, and confirming the Word with signs following." The signs did not bring faith; it was faith which brought about the signs and wonders. The Bible only says here that the Lord confirmed His word. This meant that whatever the apostles preached, the Lord performed. These mighty acts of God could not have come without faith in the Word which was spoken.

You cannot combat Satan by pointing out your past experiences to him. You can remind him of the very moment you were converted, Spirit-filled, or about the last time you received an anointed touch from God or about a certain victory you had over a problem in your life. He'll only laugh at you as you attempt to defend your faith by trying to convince him of what you believe. He already knows what you do or do not believe. At that point you are so uncertain of your faith that you resort to proving yourself to Satan when you don't owe him the time of day. You're trying to convince the author of doubt that you have faith over his doubts but you'll never succeed in doing so by pointing out past experiences to him. Faith is perfect confidence in God and when you have this confidence you will not have to defend your cause.

Faith that is built upon the foundations of feelings and past experiences is like the man who built his house upon the sand. The foundation will give way when you need its firmness the most.

When Satan came to Jesus in Matthew 4, how did Christ overcome him? Remember, if you will, that Christ's feelings were at their lowest. Forty days and nights had passed without food and his whole body and mind craved for a piece of bread. At this moment, feelings could not produce overcoming faith and neither could past experiences. Christ could have reminded Satan of who He was but He knew that Satan knew Him already and for Him to engage in an argument with Satan would only be trifle. Christ, as in every other example of life, laid the foundation of victory for every Christian believer by revealing that the only foundation for faith is the written Word of God. It's the truth that sets us free, not experiences or feelings. To build the right kind of faith you must build on the truths of God's word.

FAITH FOR EVERYDAY LIVING

Remember, faith is perfect confidence in God. This means that whatever God says is not to be questioned. No questioning, no wavering, no wondering, just accepting. We must have this perfect confidence in God's promises for everyday living and not just for church going.

Have you ever noticed that with every performed miracle in God's Word, it was preceded with a promise? God acts according to his promise. This means that you are at liberty to remind him of his promises although He needs no reminding. He doesn't act because of your needs. He doesn't act upon pity. He doesn't act because you're afflicted or in jeopardy. He acts because of his promise. The Word of God is filled with promises from God that He will not fail to perform. It is because of these promises that He will act when we call upon him.

Now the blueprint begins. Psalms 37:5, "Commit thy ways unto the Lord, trust in Him, and He shall bring it to pass."

Do you see perfect confidence in God revealed in that verse? It says, "Commit." This means to surrender, yield, give over to God ALL your ways, problems, doubts, fears and daily cares. When once a person gives something away, they no longer have it, right? Then, if we surrender our ways into the hands of God, then we no longer have our ways...but God has them.

Now, if God has them, He knows what to do about them and if you have perfect confidence in God you won't have to worry about the outcome of your "ways."

Be sure of this, that when you try to solve your problems, it means that you still have them…you haven't committed them to God. Because you still have them, they will be an even greater problem for you.

I'm sure you've seen people who tried to "make ends meet." You've probably been one of such people yourself. But did you know that you intruded into God's business when you did so? Sometime ago, God revealed to me a very simple and yet profound truth. He said, "Your business is to build my kingdom, and my business is to take care of you." This was so simple and yet this ample revelation has changed my life. Every time I found myself trying to work out my own problems, I ended in failure. But when I concentrated upon God's work and left my problems to Him, everything worked out just right.

Are we not the children of God? Didn't Christ say that He knew more about taking care of his children than we did about caring for our children? Didn't He say that God gave better gifts to his children than we give to ours? This is so simple. Our problems belong to God, our Father. Our needs belong to him because we are his.

Many people start out right. They'll tell God about

their need and ask him to make a way to solve that problem but they won't stop there. They not only want to tell God about their problem but they want to tell him how and when to do it. Now I ask you, if they know so much about the how and when and where, why do they bother God with the problems, why don't they just work it out themselves?

God doesn't need your ideas for He has ways of his own that are higher than our ways. He will not settle for anything less than total commitment. He is as an attorney taking your case and He doesn't want your case unless you're willing to turn the entire situation over to him.

After David's charge to commit our ways unto the Lord, he followed this great truth with, "...and trust also in Him." There is absolutely no need to place your ways into God's hands if you're going to continue to wonder or worry about them. You already know that God's ways are higher than your ways and His thoughts than your thoughts. You know He holds the key to every situation and the answer to every problem. Therefore, you have nothing to fear...so, trust him. Have perfect faith in Him, perfect confidence, willing to except the outcome as He will perfect it.

How wonderful is this scripture in Psalms 37:5. After committing our ways to God and trusting in Him, David gives us the perfect conclusion: "...and He shall bring it to pass." How simple! You will learn that God never answers when you want him to, but when He gets ready and He's never late. The sooner you learn this fact, the less of your patience will wear.

Don't say that you don't have faith because you do. Everyone who is a Christian has a certain amount of faith. Were this not true, then you would not be a born again child of God. It was by and through faith that you accepted the work of atonement for your sins. 1 John 1:9 promised that "If we confess our sins, He is faithful and just to forgive us our sins." Now, so far, in that scripture there is no justification. It simply promises that if you confess your sins that God would forgive you of your sins. But the real work of the atonement cannot act until you believe that promise up to this point. God says that if you confess that He would forgive. And that is what you did. You confessed your sins. You didn't wait to see if there was change in your life…you acted upon that promise with faith. You confessed and you believed that God forgave you just like he promised to do. Now, the rest of that scripture says "…and to cleanse you from all unrighteousness." Here is where the atonement met its demand and purpose. Now we know why Romans 5:1 says, "Therefore being justified by faith, we have peace with God through our Lord Jesus Christ."

It took your faith to bring you salvation and that same faith has kept you in God's grace. This is why the Word declares, "The just shall live by faith" and "…for we walk by faith and not by sight." Faith is there and it's God given.

There are two kinds of faith. One we call "Seed Faith" that was given to you of God according to Romans 12:3 which says that God "hath dealt to every man a measure of faith." Then there is a "Gift of Faith" mentioned in 1 Corinthians 12:9 which is a divine gift that is motivated by the Holy Ghost and can only be manifested through a Spirit-filled person as it is one of the gifts of the Spirit.

Now this seed of faith is like any other seed in that it must be cultivated in the right way before it will grow and produce. You have a measure of God-given faith and it is now up to you to build and to strengthen it upon the right foundation...the Word of God.

OUR APPROACH TO GOD

The way you approach God in presenting your petitions to him can make all the difference in the world. Technical as it may seem, a little thought here will prove this out. Think now for a moment. What if you were to ask your employer for a raise in salary? How would you go about it? Would you walk into his office without first knocking? Would you take your seat on the top of his desk instead of a chair? Of course not! Your absurd actions would be more detrimental to you than anything could be.

The Bible itself teaches us that there is a proper approach when coming into the presence of God. It is found in Hebrews 11:6. "He that cometh to God [*approaches God*], must believe that He is [*that He exists, that He is a reality, that He really is there in person*] and that He is a rewarder of them that diligently seek Him." There you have it: the perfect approach to the throne of God and into His presence.

He is not to be treated as a gamble. Some people come into his presence as though they aren't sure that He's there. When it comes time to pray, they're not so sure that there's a God listening, but just in case there might be, they send up a little prayer. They're like the gambler who puts his money in the slot machine and waits to see if anything comes out. The chances are a hundred to one that nothing will come about with this kind of attitude and approach. The Bible says that you must believe that He is and that He is a rewarder.

CONDITIONING THE MIND

The mind is a tremendous thing and God dwells there. It is a fact that the average human being uses only 10% of his brain. This means that the other 90% is like a huge continent of unexplored land that holds a potential too great to fathom.

But the mind is like the complex computer that must be programmed. It must be trained and conditioned by the Word of God. For that mind to believe, it will have to be conditioned to dispel doubts and everything negative. After all, faith lives where doubts are absent. But it cannot entertain faith as long as it thinks, talks, and acts upon things that are contrary to the Word of God. These things of course are promoted by Satan. This is his job.

Mark, chapter 9 records a tremendous lesson on mind conditioning. While Christ, Peter, James and John were on the mountain called the "Mount of Transfiguration," the remaining disciples were faced with the task of rebuking the powers of devils in a small child. This they had failed in doing. We must say that they failed because God never fails. When Jesus returned from the mountain, the child was brought to him for healing. Jesus said to the father of the child, "If thou canst believe all things are possible to him that believeth." Now hear the answer from that discouraged father. "Lord, I believe; help thou mine unbelief." Does this mean that one can believe and doubt at the same time? Not so. Both are enemies one to the other. Faith and doubt cannot abide in the same house. One and only one can be master. But it does appear that this man believed and doubted at the same time. But take the situation into consideration. Let's see just what has happened to provoke such a statement as this. You must consider that this man had just witnessed failure on the part of the disciples. Perhaps he had even taken his son to others in the past who had also failed. But now he faces Jesus Christ, a man who has never failed and he wants to believe with all of his heart and you can see him trying with all the strength that he has and what he is actually saying here is,

"Lord, I believe in you but help me to forget about these past failures." You see, it's difficult for you to exercise productive faith as long as you allow your mind to ponder on past failures, which were not on God's part but on yours.

Some sick folks try out evangelists just the way they would try out an automobile. If they don't get healing from one, they try another. How foolish! Those evangelists are not failing but they, the sick, are. What they are actually doing is looking for some preacher who has so much faith until his faith will override their mounting doubts. They're searching in vain for even Jesus Christ couldn't heal that type of people.

That mind has got to be conditioned to the truth that whatever God says is true. No matter what the symptoms, no matter how bad one looks, no matter what people say, God's promises should be enough. Forget about past failures, don't talk about your symptoms, and don't listen to negative statements. This is the best way to build faith. Just starve out the devil of doubt.

When Christ realized that this man's doubts was in the past failures of man and that now his faith was directed to him, He said, "Thou dumb and deaf spirit, I charge thee, come out of him, and enter no more in Him," and the child was immediately made whole. Verse 28 reveals the bewildered disciples who were astonished as to why they were unable to do the same thing as Christ had just done. Then Christ informed them that "This kind can come forth by nothing but by prayer and fasting." It was evident that they had walked with Christ which indicates that a person may have an intimate experience with Christ and still not know just how to release the faith power within. Fasting conditions the mind to channel itself into complete surrender to the will and promises of God.

THE POSITIVE MIND

With the mind cleansed from all doubts, it must be positive. God's Word is the final authority and it matters not what the circumstances may be, God's Word is still the truth which sets men free and that positive mind accepts these facts without question.

To understand the fullness of this master plan of this faith building blueprint, settle your mind to this one fantastic fact: you only believe the part of God's Word that you put into action. The rest of it you just mentally assent to it. Faith is action, not just thinking. The part of God's promises which you act upon is the only part in which you really believe!

One of the greatest scriptures in the Bible to prove this is Mark 11:24. "What things soever ye desire, when ye pray, believe that ye receive them, and ye shall have them." Did you really notice those words carefully? Did you see that God not only meets our needs but our desires of heart as well? This reminds me of my childhood days when my father bought me a little red wagon. I didn't need it but he got it for me just the same. You see, my father went beyond my needs and gave me the desires of my heart because he loved me and this is even a greater truth with our father in heaven. God wants his children to depend upon him. You are not a burden to the heavenly father. You must understand this. He wants your cry of help. This is his joy. Christ said, "It is your Father's good pleasure to give unto you the kingdom." (Luke 12:32) Therefore if the Father is pleased with doing good things for his children, feel your liberty to call upon him.

"When ye pray, *believe that ye receive*... (Mark 11:24, *emphasis mine*) This is not a future reference. This indicates that you should accept your answered prayer the moment that it is prayed. He did not say, "shall receive," which indicates a future date, but believe that ye receive at that very moment. Here's where perfect faith is being formed. If God promised to answer your prayers and to meet your request, then the moment you ask him, your prayer is just as much answered as it ever will be, because of the promise. It's like putting a letter in the mail box. You can say I've answered so and so with this letter. It may be two days before they get it but as far as you're concerned it's already answered.

The real stumbling block to perfect faith is revealed in 1 Corinthians 2:14: "But the natural man receiveth not the things of the Spirit of God: for they are foolishness unto him: neither can he know them, because they are spiritually discerned."

If there is a natural man who cannot receive the things of God, then we may assume that there is a spirit man within us who can receive divine revelations from God's Words and understand them. However, to understand the spirit man we would have to acquaint ourselves with the natural man and find out just what makes him tick.

Now, here is an interesting observation: How was Adam educated? Have you ever given this any thought? Adam never was taught any language nor did he have to learn the difference between hot and cold; black and white; the sky and the sea; why birds flew and fish swam. Adam knew all things from the day that he was created. What a blessing! He was a "brain" from his first day on earth until his last.

You see, there was a reason behind this. The secret is found in Genesis 2:7. "And the Lord God formed man of the dust of the ground, and breathed into his nostrils the breath of life; and man became a living soul." Here is the only place in the scriptures which states that God put anything into man...his breath. Any way you want to look at this scripture there is one fact that remains...God breathed into Adam and that breath caused him to be not only an existing being but an eternal soul. Whatever the purpose of God's breath in Adam, the facts remain that an educated being came into existence which did not have to be taught about life and all the new things in life that God had just created. Therefore, it must be assumed that God's breath, being a part of him, was in fact a part of God himself breathed into man.

Children that are born into today's world are not blessed with this immediate knowledge and education. But they do possess five wonderful servants which can teach them the things that they need to learn. We call these five servants our five senses. Through these channels we learn everything that we now know. Through the trial and error method, our sense of touch tells us what is hot or cold; what is rough or smooth; what is wet or dry. Our sense of taste, through the trial and error method educates us to know the difference between the taste of meat and the taste of potatoes. And on goes the story. But Adam never needed these faculties to learn until after he had disobeyed God.

That part of God that was breathed into Adam still remains in man today but because of Adam's transgression, that spirit man has been suppressed by the carnal man who needs and uses the five senses to learn and reason. The worst part of this story is that man has learned to rely so greatly upon his five senses for his learning until he will not believe in anything that his senses will not respond to. Here is the discord between the natural man and the spirit man: something inside you wants to rely solely upon the truths of God's Word but the carnal mind still wants to reason a thing out before it believes. Therefore, "common sense," as we call it, which in reality is the carnal mind, can be the evil force which thwarts our faith and hinders our receiving answers to prayers and deliverances to our afflictions. Thus, we're now carried back to the roots.

Moffatt's translation of Hebrews 11:1 says, "Faith is when we're convinced that we have that which we cannot see." Here is faith based solely upon the Word. You see according to your senses, a thing may or may not be possible, and as far as that is concerned, it may not even be reasonable. But because God says it is possible, the spirit man accepts the possibility as a fact.

Now back to Mark 11:24: "Whatsoever things ye desire, when ye pray believe that ye receive them...and ye shall have them." From the moment you ask God for a thing to be done, you accept it as done. Not because of any evidence that you have seen, felt, heard, tasted or smelled, but because God's Word is truth in the face of all contradiction. This is like mailing your house or car payment. The moment you place that envelope in the mailbox, that payment has been made as far as you're concerned. It hasn't reached its destination, and the payment has not yet been accredited to your account, but your faith in the mail service justifies your confidence that the payment is just as good as paid.

Your prayer has been sent. Is there any reason for you to question whether or not it will be received in God's throne room? 1 John 5:15 says, "And if we know that he hear us, whatsoever we ask, we know that we have the petitions that we desired of him." There you have it. *If we know* that he hears us! Is there any reason why he should not hear us? According to his Word, He always hears. We can safely assume that the mail always goes through and that our prayers are accredited to our account and that not one goes unheard or unnoticed.

Perfect confidence in the word! This is faith. First John is filled with this definition on faith. Here it is again in 1 John 3:21-22 (emphasis mine): "Beloved, if our heart condemns us not, then have we *confidence* toward God. And whatsoever we ask, we *receive* of him, because we keep his commandments, and do those things that are pleasing in his sight." Here it is again, "And this is the *confidence* that we have in him, that, if we ask anything according to his will, he heareth us." (1 John 5:14, emphasis mine).

Since it is always the simple things that confound our little minds, let's take a simple scripture, Matthew 7:7: "Ask and ye shall receive." That's great, isn't it? But what about the following verse which is far greater? It says, "And to everyone that asketh, receiveth." (Matthew 7:8) Which do you believe is greater? No matter how difficult this is to believe, it is still the Word, the Living Word, the True Word. This is God's promise to you and to me. If he says that *everyone* receiveth that asketh, then I have no reason to question God.

A prayer has been prayed. The Word says that that prayer has been answered. But the carnal mind looks up with its eyes to *see* if there is any evidence of an answered prayer. The carnal mind *listens* to hear if there is an answered prayer. The carnal mind reaches out to *feel* if there is any evidence of an answered prayer And because he cannot *feel*, *touch* or *see*, he refuses to believe. He turns off to the promise of God's Word. He ignores the fact that God cannot lie. He says that he believes, but refuses to accept anything that the five senses cannot fathom. But the spirit man within, who knows the ways of God, can see and hear the answered prayer because the evidence that he depends upon is God's Word.

When you come to the end of reasoning and you stand at the edge of the cliff, your senses have become exhausted and your reasoning has failed, faith in the Word reaches out and brings that which you could not see into the realms of the natural because you believed without sense knowledge evidence. The only evidence that you need is the unfailing Word.

Hebrews 11:1, "Now faith is a substance of things hoped for, the evidence of things not seen." That scripture will never mean anything to you until you fathom the two key words, "substance" and "evidence." Faith is not a fantasy nor is it wishful thinking. It is a substance. It is real and tangible. It's just as real as a piece of wood. The only difference is that at first it is latent, meaning that it exists but cannot be seen and will not be seen until one believes.

How can I believe, you say, if I don't see? Well

friend, if you could see, why would you need to believe? It doesn't take faith to believe in something that we can see, feel or hear. But when you believe (because of the Word), although you cannot see the evidence, and you accept your prayer as answered, then the material answer will come to you and will then become the evidence of those things which before you could not see.

The story goes that a young man stood on a river bank questioning whether or not he could swim the broad river that stretched before him. He decided that he could make it. At the half way point he lost faith in his judgment and turned and went back. This is a perfect image of those who profess faith in a certain matter and then back away from their profession when the going gets tough.

But Hebrews 10:23 has the answer for the halfway, faith-wavering swimmer: "Let us hold fast our profession of faith without wavering; for He is faithful that promised." If you profess to have faith in a matter, that faith will have to be in God's ability and not yours. So just because the waters get rough at the halfway point, is no reason to give up and say, "Well, I don't suppose I had enough faith after all." This would be all that Satan would want to hear. You're defeated at that point. But the scripture declares here that you should "...hold fast your profession of faith, without wavering..." This means forgetting the doubts, leave them behind, no questioning...plunge ahead. Why?

"...because He is faithful that promised."

BUILDING YOUR DOUBTS

There is such a thing as building your doubt and many Christians do it all the time. They hold to the old adage, "If once you don't succeed, try, try and try again." This doesn't work with God. Matthew 7:7 says, "Ask, and you shall receive." That's all there is to it. Go your way with perfect confidence and the prayer is answered. There is no need to go back and ask God again for something that you know that He heard the first time. God is not hard of hearing. The Bible says that his "...ear is not dull of hearing." Each time you ask God over again for the same thing, you're only building doubt in your mind. Remember that we said that after we commit our ways unto the Lord, we go our way "...trusting also in Him."

When you hold a dollar bill in your hand, what do you see? Money? Read what it says. It's a certificate. That's all. It certifies that the government has an equal amount of gold banked to cover the face value of that certificate. But do you question it? Of course not and neither does the lady in the store who works behind the counter.

God's Word is a certificate and He, himself, backs it up. Shouldn't that be enough for you? Take God's Word like a blank check and fill in the amount and God will have to back it up. This is why we say that your prayers are just as good as money in the bank.

They're answered the moment you send in the request. Your holding fast a profession of faith will soon yield the "...evidence of things not seen." This is faith for everyday living.

FAITH FOR HEALING AND DELIVERANCE

A person can never obtain deliverance from fear or an affliction until he's convinced that it is God's will to set him free. Many are suffering unduly at this moment because they believe that it is God's will for them to be afflicted. They try to justify their doubts and lack of faith and attempt to convince you that there are times when it is God's will for his children to be sick. This they do by using various incidents in the Bible.

The simplest form of reasoning will show you just how ridiculous this belief really is. Jesus said that the heavenly father gave better gifts to his children than did earthly fathers. Do you believe this? Do you get glory out of seeing your children sick? Could you enjoy seeing your child die with some incurable disease? Of course not. Then how can we imagine a kind, loving God glorying from seeing his children afflicted?

"But how am I to know God's will," you ask? Look in the right place. Where? In His will. That's right! When Christ died on Calvary, He left us a will. It's the New Testament. That's what the word "testament" means...a "will." Whatever you read in that will is for you. If it says, "By His stripes ye were healed," then that promise was *willed* to you by Jesus Christ himself.

In Psalms 103:3 the Bible says, "Who forgiveth all thine iniquities; who healeth all thy diseases." Here are the two principle provisions in the atonement: *healing* and *salvation*. The death of Christ on Calvary provided these two things. Therefore, if the atonement made provision for salvation, it also made provision for healing. Is it always God's will to save the sinner? Do we question the will of God when a sinner comes forward to be saved? Certainly not! How foolish it would be to cry, "Lord, save this sinner, *if* it be thy will." We already know that it's God's will to save because salvation was provided in the atonement. If we're definite of this, then, why do we question the will of God in divine healing? You must be convinced by God's Word that it is always his will to heal.

Still willing to justify their lack of faith, many people will cling to the story of Job. Job was afflicted, they say, because it was God's will. This is not true. It was not God's will for Job to be afflicted and He certainly didn't receive any glory out of watching Job suffer. God "allowed" Satan to bring the affliction upon Job but Job had it coming to him. It was Job, himself, who opened the door of opportunity for Satan to bring these afflictions upon him. That door of opportunity was opened because of one word: *fear*.

Now there are a few things at this point that you should understand. Satan has no claims or rights upon you whatsoever. There is a hedge about you and everything that you possess just as it was about Job. Within that hedge is righteous territory and that territory is off limits to Satan and he knows this. But what's more important is that you know it. Frankly, most people don't and Satan knows this. Therefore, he cannot reach either you or your possessions without entering the hedge that God has placed around you. Still, he doesn't give up. Some way, somehow he must devise a way of entering this forbidden territory of your life. He cannot open up the hedge and he knows that God will never do it, thus, the only way that hedge can be opened is by you and you alone.

From Matthew 12:44 we know that Satan has learned through the thousands of years of existence and through practice that he can deceive a person and blind them from knowing their lawful rights in the Redemptive work of Calvary. In this verse (44) he is still claiming a born again person as "...my house" when it doesn't belong to him at all. But he is trying to plant a seed of doubt within this person, causing him to doubt his experience with God and thereby opening up the hedge for him to return into the house that once was his.

Fear is the key to the opening of the hedge that is around you. This was the key that opened the hedge around Job. As far as his life was concerned, it was untarnished. He was a perfect man and served God in every way he knew. He was not a superman. He was not a genius. His perfection was only in his service and devotion to God. Had he been a genius, he would have known more than what he did. With all of his religious perfection, he still did not know God's will for his life. He wasn't aware that prosperity was God's will for his life. He confessed that he believed that God had given all of his possessions to him but he wasn't convinced that God would let him keep it. His idea was that he was just a lucky man thus far, whose luck would finally run out because there was a devil walking about within the earth that would sooner or later take everything away from him. Had he known God's will for his life, he would never have had need to fear for the loss of his family or his earthly possessions. But calamity did strike. The enemy had entered the forbidden territory. The hedge about him had been penetrated, but how? Job himself gives the answer to this question. Now that everything had been taken from him, he confesses to the cause of it. He says, (Job 3:25, 26) "For the thing which I greatly feared is come upon me, and that which I was afraid of is come unto me. I was not in safety, neither had I rest, neither was I quiet; yet trouble came." In the first chapter, verse 21, we have proof that Job didn't know the will of God. He only knew half of it. He knew that everything he had was given of God, but he didn't know that it was Satan who took it all away and here he claims that God had taken it away.

Job's fear didn't begin at the first news of calamity. Job 3:26 reveals him to be a man who lived in fear of losing what he had. He confesses here that he didn't feel safe and that he lived without rest. In verse 25 he reveals that the very things that happened to him were the things that he had been afraid would happen. His own fear which was caused by his lack of knowledge of God's will was the very thing that opened the hedge for Satan to enter forbidden territory.

Fear and insecurity are caused by the lack of confidence (faith) in God which in turn is caused by a lack of knowledge as to God's will concerning you. Job was perfect in his service to God but he didn't know God's will for his life. He took his success as "luck." He expected the worse and his expectations opened the "hedge."

Both Job and Satan learned great lessons in this confrontation. Satan learned that he only multiplies God's blessings on his children when he attempts to subtract them. Job learned that it was God's will for him to prosper, to live in peace without fear and that if anything did come against him, that God would turn curses into blessings as long as he kept the faith.

You cannot be healed until you know and realize that it is God's will. As long as you question the fact, my prayers or the prayers of any other evangelist will never destroy your doubts which hinder your deliverance. When I pray for anyone who wants healing, I first ask them if they believe it is God's will. If they don't believe it is God's will to heal them, then I'm wasting my time and theirs.

We have two wills: the Old Testament and the New Testament. Both declare that it is God's will (it's in the will) to heal. Healing was in the will according to Job 33:24, 25, "Then he is gracious unto him, and saith, Deliver him from going down to the pit: I have found a ransom (healing). His flesh shall be fresher than a child's: he shall return to the days of his youth."

It was God's will to heal those who were plagued in Numbers 21:9 and the same is revealed in Isaiah 53. Never can you give scriptural evidence that it is God's will for you to suffer. Christ went to the cross to carry your sicknesses and your pain in order that you may live free from these things. The atonement on the cross was for two purposes: to redeem from sin and to set free from sickness. Both of these are the results of the curse that Satan brought about in Eden.

Isaiah 53 is probably the greatest chapter in the Bible on the redemptive work of Christ. Let's read it: "Who hath believed our report? and to whom is the arm of the Lord revealed? For he shall grow up before him as a tender plant, and as a root out of a dry ground; he hath no form nor comeliness; and when we shall see him, there is no beauty that we should desire him. He is despised and rejected of men; a man of sorrows, and acquainted with grief; and we hid as it were our faces from him; he was despised, and we esteemed him not. Surely he hath borne our griefs, and carried our sorrows: yet we did esteem him stricken smitten of God, and afflicted. But he was wounded for our transgressions, he was bruised for our iniquities: the chastisement of our peace was upon him; and with his stripes we are healed. All we like sheep have gone astray; we have turned every one to his own way; and the Lord hath laid upon him the iniquity of us all. He was oppressed, and he was afflicted, yet he opened not his mouth: he is brought as a lamb to the slaughter, and as a sheep before her shearers is dumb, so he openeth not his mouth. He was taken from prison and from judgment: and who shall declare his generation? for he was cut off out of the land of the living: for the transgression of my people was he stricken. And he made his grave with the wicked, and with the rich in his death; because he had done no violence, neither was any deceit in his mouth. Yet it pleased the Lord to bruise him; he hath put him to grief: when thou shalt make his soul an offering for sin, he shall see his seed, he shall prolong his days, and the pleasure of the Lord shall prosper in his hand. He shall see of the travail of his soul, and shall be satisfied: by his knowledge shall my righteous servant justify many; for he shall bear their iniquities. Therefore will I divide him a portion with the great, and he shall divide the spoil with the strong; because he hath poured out his soul unto death: and he was numbered with the transgressors; and he bare the sin of many, and made intercession for the transgressors."

My, what a chapter! It contains the beginning and the end with life in the middle. This chapter contains redemption through the shed blood of Jesus Christ from verse 1 through to verse 12. This chapter offers forgiveness of sins, remission of sins and abolishment of sicknesses and disease. It offers life both here and in the hereafter. It offers health and prosperity in the life present. It's all here in the projected new will. Although this is the Old Testament (the old will) crying out, it is prophecy of the new will which makes it the same as the new will.

Isaiah 53 is not accepted by many to refer to physical healing. It is claimed that the entire chapter is devoted to the healing of the soul, spiritual healing, and that no physical deliverance is promised. However, these false ideas can be easily contradicted without question.

Surely he hath borne our "griefs" and carried our "sorrows" is a mistranslation. These Hebrews words, "choli and makob" are rendered in the original text as disease and sickness. They are rendered correctly in Deut. 7:15; 28:61; 1 Kings-17:17; 2 Kings 1:2; 8:8; 2 Chron. 16:12; 21:15. The word "makob" is "pain" in Job 14:22; 33:19. You may check any commentary on these translations for confirmation. But no better commentary can be found than that of Matthew in chapter 8:16, 17.

Here is that translation of Matthew. "When the even was come, they brought unto him many that were possessed with devils: and he cast out the spirits with his word, and healed all that were sick: That it might be fulfilled which was spoken by Esaias (Isaiah 53) the prophet, saying, Himself took our infirmities, and bare our sicknesses."

This is proof that the redemptive plan of Isaiah 53 covered healing for the physical body the same as for the spiritual healing for the soul.

THE ROLE OF THE MIND

When do we receive our healing? The moment that we ask for it. When do we receive anything from God? The moment that we ask for it. Only one thing can prevent the tangibility of an answered prayer and that is a thing called doubt. Doubt is not a disease. Doubt is not a thing. Doubt is a mistranslation of the mental impulses. If this sounds confusing to you, let's make it simple. Have your eyes ever played tricks on you and caused you to see things that didn't exist? Of course they have. Mine have. As a matter of fact mine have played more tricks on me lately than ever before. It hasn't been due to old age because I'm a young man. But due to extensive traveling and pushing myself while driving; I have begun to have illusions at night when I have forced myself to stay awake while driving. I see people walking in front of my car and I immediately slam on my brakes only to find that there was no one there. I have seen trucks in front of me that didn't exist. I saw things that never existed.

Have you ever thought you heard something when no one else heard the sound? Have you ever tasted a thing and it actually tasted like something else? Or perhaps there were times when you couldn't taste at all. Then there were times when you thought you smelled something that actually never gave off a scent to begin with. So right here, you have confessed that at least four of your five senses have, at one time or another, lied to you. They have faltered. They have failed to interpret your nerve impulses properly. Thus, if four of these servants have failed, who is to say that all five have been guilty of doing the same thing? You cannot always believe your five senses. Over and over they have proven to be unreliable. But you continue to believe them and this is why you have doubts when it comes to the spiritual.

"Defecting" your senses is the only way that Satan can make you doubt God's healing touch. You have only one thing to rely on and that is the promise of God's Word that "everyone that asketh receiveth." The symptoms of your past ailments can be so mentally strong until it would be so easy to confess that you were still sick and still in pain. But fathom this if you will, if you're still sick, then God's Word is not true, and if it isn't true then we can no longer believe John 3:16 and the other salvation scriptures of the Bible. We are hopeless because the promises of the Word are not reliable. God cannot lie, He has never lied and He will never lie. He cannot go back upon his promises. Therefore we can only conclude that when you ask God for healing, He does it that very moment. If you say that you can still feel the pain, how do you know but that it is Satan warping and defecting your sense of touch so as to cause you to confess that you were not healed? Then of course when he gets that confession out of you, it will only open the door to let the real thing come back in again. Here is the difference between healing and deliverance. You receive your healing the moment that you ask for it. If you will accept God's Word for what it is, *truth*, then you will believe that you have received your healing no matter what kind of mental symptoms Satan tries to tag on you. Remember, your senses can lie to you and seem so real in doing so. But when you defy your senses and confess that God's Word is truth and every man a liar, including Satan, Satan will be unable to continue his bombardment upon your senses. When you have overcome him, you have received your deliverance. But whatever you do, confess your healing the moment you ask God for it. You can do it without speaking falsely. The Bible says that a man confesses with his mouth what he believes in his heart. Put your faith into action and confess with your mouth that God has healed you and hold on to that confession.

So many people defeat their own testimony. They'll come forward for prayer and afterwards they'll ask you to keep on praying for them. Why? Didn't God hear the first time? Is he hard of hearing? Was He busy with someone else when the first prayer was prayed? Why ask God a second or third time for something that He heard the first time? His promises are true. This is what the writer of Hebrews was talking about when he said, "Let us hold fast our PROFESSION of faith without wavering [*don't change in the middle of the stream*], for he is faithful that promised." Once again, we see God answering prayer, not because you have a need, but because He promised. God operates because He promised. He isn't honoring you because He feels sorry for you, but because He made you a promise and He will always keep his promises.

Mark 11:24 now becomes even more real: "Whatsoever things ye desire, when you pray, believe that ye receive them." There's no waiting period here. He says to believe that ye receive at the very moment that you pray. You don't have to worry whether or not your confession is true when you say you are healed, you can say it upon the authority of God's promises. Confess it. Confess your healing. Confess your answered prayer. The more you confess it, the more you believe it and the more you believe it, the less chance Satan has to hold his deceiving symptoms on you. He has to go. He cannot bind you when he sees that you have a made up mind to confess victory. His doubts will have to go. His symptoms will have to vanish. He is defeated, he has always been defeated and he will always be the defeated one. He has no power except that you let him have. He's a loser. With Christ, you're a winner! Think about that. All of this time, Satan has pulled the wool over your eyes. You have been prayed for time and again and thought that God didn't hear your prayer when all the same time Satan was substituting fake, mental symptoms to cause you to believe that you were not healed and thereby bringing the old affliction back upon you. You were healed. You were healed every time you were prayed for because God always fulfills his promises. But you would not confess your healing. You believed the lying symptoms of Satan. You had your healing over sickness but never received deliverance over the doubts that Satan manufactured in your mind. Now forget about your past. Realize your mistakes in believing the devil and put your trust in the Lord. Confess your victory and your healing before men and see Satan lose the battle.

A THORN IN THE FLESH

I have been amazed through the years of preaching as to how many preachers preach that sickness is a blessing. In almost every case I have noticed a misfortune or sickness in their own lives which reveal the motive behind their preaching. Unwilling to accept God's Word for what it says, they set out to justify their failures. They want to justify their sicknesses and thus they say that sickness is a blessing.

When have you ever read that God receives glory out of suffering? You won't find it in God's Word unless you twist it to pieces and then if you do, it is no longer God's Word. Take any example in the Bible of suffering and show me where God was glorified. You won't be able to use the blind man of John 9. Christ received no glory out of watching this poor helpless creature stumble about the temple to seek someone to lead him across the street. The only thing that Christ receives glory from in these situations is delivering such people and setting them free, giving them new life and new hope and that is just what He did in this case.

Another great crutch is 2 Corinthians 12:7-10. No example in the Bible is more used than this one to prove sickness as a blessing. This example is not only used by the ignorant and the unlearned but by learned and scholarly men. Clergymen who have doctorate titles preceding their names have poorly used this scripture to preach justified sickness and to make the atonement of no effect. All sorts of stories are told about the many afflictions of the great apostle Paul. Some hold that he had an incurable disease while others contest that he had poor eyesight.

It is true that Paul confessed to having "a thorn in the flesh," but it is also true that he plainly revealed to us what that thorn in the flesh was so we would not have to speculate. And yet speculate is just the very thing that many are doing. Firstly, let's look at the background and the reasons for Paul going into this discourse.

Paul was a mighty preacher and to him was given many revelations by the Lord (2 Corinthians 12:7). Evidently God revealed more divine secrets to this man than usual. This unusual contact with God could have easily provoked him to pride and exaltation. Because of this Paul says, "...there was given unto me a thorn in the flesh." Not only does Paul here mention the purpose of this "thorn," but he also reveals clearly what it was. "...and lest I should be exalted above measure through the abundance of the revelations, there was given unto me a thorn in the flesh, the messenger of Satan..." Here the mystery is answered. The word "messenger" here is translated from the Greek "aggelos," meaning "an angel from or of Satan." This indicated that Satan had assigned one special devil to follow the apostle wherever he went to "...buffet me, lest I should be exalted above measure."

What a terrible thought...to have a special devil to follow you wherever you went. This thing was so vexing until Paul sought the Lord three times (verse 8) to deliver him from his unwanted company. These vexing spirits will always be accompanying us just as it was with Paul. God never promised Paul to take away the "thorn," instead he gave Paul a special promise: "And He said unto me, My grace is sufficient for thee: for my strength is made perfect in weakness.

Most gladly therefore will I rather glory in my infirmities, that the power of Christ may rest upon me." (2 Cor. 12:9)

Paul continues, "Therefore I take pleasure in infirmities..." (2 Cor. 12:10) What a statement for Paul to make if his "thorn" and "infirmities" were physical afflictions. How could one praise God for cancer? How could one see God being glorified from seeing one of his children walking around blind, seeking for someone to lead them? How could one glory in being plagued with an incurable disease? If sickness glorifies God, then why have healing services for people to be healed? If sickness glorifies God, then why don't we have prayer lines to ask God to smite us all with cancer so as to glorify him? This is absolutely absurd!

"Infirmities" here is translated from the word "asthenes" (Gr.) meaning "weakness or without strength." For one to see why Paul was weak and without strength at this time he would only have to read the preceding chapter (2 Cor. 11:23-28). Notice these infirmities which composed Paul's "thorn in the flesh."

1. Stripes above measure. (vs. 23)
2. In prison more often. (vs. 23)
3. Beaten with rods three times. (vs. 25)
4. Beaten with stripes five times. (vs. 24)
5. Once was stoned. (vs. 25)
6. Suffered shipwreck three times. (vs. 25)

7. Spent a day and night floating in the ocean. (vs. 25)

8. Journeyings often; in perils of waters, perils of robbers, perils of his countrymen, perils by the heathen, perils in the city, in perils in the wilderness, in perils in the sea, in perils among false brethern. (vs. 26)

9. In weariness and painfulness, watchings often, in hunger and thirst, in fasting often, in cold and nakedness. (vs. 27)

10. Beside the   daily cares and the care of the churches. (vs. 28)

Now Paul concludes his listing of these cares and sorrows that were upon him, but listen now as he confirms our statements concerning the "infirmities." "If I must need glory, I will glory of the things which concern mine infirmities." (vs. 30)

It is said that this great warrior of the faith had better than 2,000 scars upon his body which he had suffered "for the gospel's sake." Yet, we hear him say that God's strength in him was perfected by his weakness, i.e. these infirmities which kept him humble in the eyes of God and ever realizing that all that which he wrought was done, not of his power, but the power of Christ within him. No wonder that Paul could say, "From henceforth let no man trouble me: for I bear in my body the marks of the Lord Jesus." (Gal. 6:17) Listen to him scoff at the whimpering complainer whose feelings have been hurt by harsh words. He is saying, "Don't come to me telling me about your little trials and temptations, for I carry the marks and scars of real tribulations." Thus, Paul's "thorn" was anything but a physical sickness.

Let's hear one more verse of this: "Therefore I take pleasure in infirmities, in reproaches, in necessities, in persecutions, in distresses for Christ's sake: for when I am weak, then am I strong." (2 Cor. 12:10)

CLAIM YOUR RIGHTS

From the time that Jesus Christ lifted His head on Calvary's cross and cried "It is finished," your soul was ransomed by his death and offered back to God. You may be the son who has wasted his life and who sits in the hog pen feeding the swine, but you still belong as much to the father as does the son who stayed home. You're not eating around the father's table, wearing sandals or a gold ring, but you're still his, all because of Calvary's offering.

Satan has blinded people from their rights in Calvary. They are being cheated out of things that already belong to them. God's Word declares that they have been bought with a price. They belong to God. Salvation for their soul has already been provided. They don't have to ask for salvation, it is already theirs for accepting it. The Bible teaches the sinner to confess his sin (1 John 1:9) but God does the rest. Salvation is theirs and must be accepted. Salvation is their golden bank account upon which they can make the eternal withdrawal at any time they are willing to forsake sin. If they want to hold on to their sin and the world, their bank account is still there just the same. They don't even have to ask for it, it has already been made out in their name. They only need to accept what is rightfully theirs which they can lay hold upon once they have made the choice to forsake sin and serve the Lord,

This same atonement made the same provisions for your healing and deliverance. Your sickness and what sicknesses that Satan may try to place upon you have already been placed upon Christ. If He took my sicknesses, then why should I accept them? If we accept sickness in spite of his suffering for us, then we are causing his suffering to be in vain. If we had to suffer anyway, then Christ's suffering was useless. But He took our sicknesses upon himself that we could live free from them. The devil will tell you that everybody gets sick and that you'll have to take your share. If you believe that, then you put stripes upon your own back and those Christ suffered were for nothing. If Christ carried your sicknesses and suffered your pains, then why must you take your afflictions and diseases back from him and suffer them yourself? You can if you want to. And this you will do if you listen to the lies of Satan who has blinded so many people of their rights in Calvary.

Isaiah 53:5 says, "With His stripes we ARE healed." This, of course, was looking forward to Calvary. But Peter looked back to Calvary and said,

"...by whose stripes ye *were* healed." (1 Pet. 2:24, *emphasis mine*). Friend, the work of Calvary has been wrought, don't make it in vain. Accept what is rightfully yours and what has been provided for you in his will.

BACK TO BASICS

I must confess. A few years ago, I was just as hard and heartless as the next preacher. I thought that I had it all squared away in my mind on what was right and what was wrong. I was God-ordained to lash out against the sins of men and women and to preach condemnation upon them.

If anyone had the straight and narrow all laid out, it was me. I thought that the harder that I preached, the more righteous I was before God. Anything less was compromising, and I just couldn't have that.

I gave no one the benefit of the doubt. I was nothing short of a Pharisee when it came to shelling out the "gospel truth." Just like the rest of my narrow-minded clan of preachers, I preached the old "get in or get out." There was no elasticity in my gospel. None whatsoever.

Was I right in preaching this way? A lot of folks thought so because they backed my ministry during those years. Have I changed? Yes, I have. Why? First of all, let me explain why I did preach that way.

We all allow ourselves to be influenced, whether we admit it or not. We'll drive down the road at a very safe and normal speed. We look through our rear view mirror and see a truck tailgating us. What do we do? I'll tell you. Instead of minding our own business and letting the tailgater do as he will, we'll speed up, and break the law, just to get away from him. What has happened is that we have allowed ourselves to be influenced into speeding by some nut who doesn't need to be on the highway to start with. If he wasn't going fast enough, that was his problem.

So our environment has molded us. We want to be popular and liked. We don't want to be a sore thumb, a stick in the mud. So, we go along with whatever the feeling of the crowd is.

I started out as a "boy evangelist." Those ministers with whom I associated were the hard-nosed type. Mine was a constant influence. I was taught, influenced, molded and guided by my religious surroundings.

You see, when one is exposed to only one thing, to just one side of the story, it becomes not just training, but brain-washing. They were hard-line preachers, so I was the same. They prided me for my so-called stand for holiness, and that only made me harder.

It wasn't until I removed myself from that kind of environment that I began to see things from an overall perspective. It was not that the Bible had changed. I had read scriptures before that I had purposely neglected to preach because they conflicted with my current mode of preaching. It wasn't that I was neglecting the truth because I passed them off as scriptures that I couldn't understand, as they didn't seem to fit what I had been taught.

THE GREAT DIVISION

The great division in the church world and among denominations has not been as a result of the governmental structure of each denomination. As a matter of fact, people don't really seem to care one way or the other as to how the organizations structure their format and network of business.

The great division is not in the political set-up and the power struggle between energetic and ambitious leaders. This does exist and everyone knows it. Without exception, every denominational organization is plagued with power struggles for position, but it has not been the principle element for dividing the body of Christ.

The love of money may be the root of all evil, and it has become a subject of controversy many times: how to get it, what to do with it, who's going to benefit from it, or who will get credit for it. But it still hasn't been the great controversy.

Does anyone ask, "What can be done for the kingdom of God?" Yes, but no one gets upset too often upon the differences of opinion. Everyone seems to have their idea as to how the world should be reached for the Lord, but it doesn't seem important enough to become divided.

THE ONE DIVIDING CONTROVERSY

What is sin? What is right and wrong? What constitutes Christian ethics and what makes a sinner a sinner? Here's where the dividing line is drawn. Here is where denominational barriers are formed and the body of Christ is divided.

Look at the numerous churches and denominations in our world right now…all using the same Bible. All claiming to be right; and yet all preaching a different doctrine with different versions. Can this possibly be right? Can God be pleased with what He sees? Is it possible that all of these churches can be right? I don't know how. Somebody has got to be right and someone has to be wrong. All problems seem to have a right and wrong solution, and it seems logical that the Bible is the same way.

Man has always been basically a rebel. If this were not true, Adam would not have brought the curse upon us. He will admit to a set of principles, to a set of rules, to certain teachings, provided that they are his own. Churches are the same way. They all will admit that there is "one way," but they want to be the "one way."

Man is basically destructive. He doesn't care to cry out for anything good, but he's ready to lash out against what he thinks to be wrong. He feels more honor in being a rebellious renegade than he does in being a constructive builder. He's a killer instead of a healer. He puts down instead of lifting up and lives by principles as long as they are his principles.

What fulfillment is there in preaching against sin alone? That's like telling someone that they're building their house all wrong but not being able to tell them how to do it right. But if one can preach the "how to do it right," the right will automatically override the wrong.

It's great to preach the love of God and deliverance from condemnation. This is what people need and what they really want to hear. But it doesn't seem to be in the nature of man to preach in this manner. This "Cry aloud and spare not" was to the prophets of old under direct commandment of the Lord for people who lived in an era when they couldn't get complete deliverance from their sins.

Today we live under grace, delivered from the bondage of sin, coerced by the love of God, and as Paul said, "I am determined not to know anything among you save Jesus Christ and Him crucified." Paul was straight forward with the idolatrous Romans, but he corrected with love and the Word. He was not excusing the Galatians and the Corinthians in their hidden sins, but he was careful to instruct with kindness.

Think about this. Wasn't this really the attitude of our Lord? He was kind and understanding. He could look upon an adulterous woman surrounded by accusers and see some good in her. He wasn't like some of our church councils today who would readily dismiss her from the local fellowship and condemn her before her time.

Some people seem to have the idea that they're either ordained of God to keep everybody straight or that God is too merciful so they have to take the situation in hand. Do you think this is overstating the truth? If so, listen to what Paul says in Romans 2:3-4: "And thinkest thou this, man, that judgest them which do such things and doest the same, that thou shalt escape the judgment of God? Or despisest thou the riches of His goodness and forbearance and long-suffering; not knowing that the goodness of God leadeth thee to repentance?"

Can you imagine this? Paul said that there were those who despise the goodness and longsuffering of God. He said that the goodness and longsuffering of God would lead to repentance.

People have the same attitude as the prophet Jonah. Jonah was a prophet of God. So, if this be so, then what were his reasons for not wanting to go to Ninevah? It was because he was a racist.

Nineveh was a Gentile city and he was a Hebrew. God had told him to go into that great city and tell them that He was going to destroy them because of their sins. But listen to Jonah's reply: He said, "Lord, if I go and tell them what you said, they'll repent in sackcloth and ashes and then you will forgive them."

You see, Jonah was willing to go and preach wrath as long as he could know that the destruction would come. But he knew the merciful heart of God. He knew that the people of Nineveh would repent and that God would forgive them.

He did finally preach to them and prophesied. The people did repent and God did forgive them and spared them. But Jonah was so mad at God that he sat outside the city crying and bellyaching and wishing himself dead because God didn't destroy Nineveh.

Can you imagine this? This is the very kind of attitude that Paul was talking about in Romans 2:3-4. Despising the mercy and longsuffering of God. This is the kind of attitude being manifested behind pulpits in our generation today. Everybody wants to dry-clean everyone else. "Don't do this, don't do that, this is wrong and that's a sin." Haven't they read that you overcome evil with good?

A SET OF RULES

Before we get right down to the basics of salvation and what is right and wrong, let's talk about guidelines.

There are two things that have always served as stumbling blocks at this point. One is called "new morality" and the other is "tradition." The new morality doctrine is a diabolical teaching. It concludes that every man should decide what is right or wrong for himself personally.

If a man knew so much about what was good and bad for him, how come he is in such bad shape today? Why even believe in God if he is going to be a God unto himself and set his own set of rules and commandments? I can see atheists and infidels embracing this doctrine, but not church people. It doesn't make any sense whatsoever. But you'll hear them say, "I don't care what the preacher preaches, I'm going to live the way I think is best for me." These kind of folks don't need a preacher. He wouldn't do them any good anyway.

Then there is that gigantic obstacle that Christ had to confront when He came preaching the Good News of the Kingdom. It's a thing we call "tradition," and it's still with us today. It's the thing that condemns people for doing things that aren't really wrong and has them doing other things that aren't really necessary.

The net of tradition is woven by people who say, "We've always done it this way, and we've always heard it preached this way, so we'll always stick with it." We've also had this very popular saying: "If it was a sin twenty years ago, it's still a sin today."

Okay, so that statement is true, but listen to the whole thing. Notice the first word, "if." "If it was a sin." Sure, sin is sin whether it was in the last century or this one, but what is sin? Just because a denomination declares a thing to be sin in their organizational teachings doesn't make it so. Just because Uncle John was a good honest man doesn't make his ideas about sin the gospel truth.

We build more walls between the Cross of Calvary and the sinner by preaching traditional sins than by any other method, and I can't see God pleased with it.

Before you get so excited on preaching against sin, first take the time to find out what sin is and stick with it. Don't forget that the Bible itself is your guide, your set of rules. You won't learn what sin is by deciding for yourself, and you won't learn anything from traditional ideas. If the Bible isn't good enough for you to find your answers, then throw it away because it's not doing you any good. But if you throw it away, you're not a Christian to begin with and this message isn't doing you any good either.

Romans 3:4 says: "Let God [the Word] be truth and every man a liar..." and that's exactly what man is if he is in disagreement with the Word.

THE BASICS OF RIGHT AND WRONG

Just how complicated is salvation anyway? Is it only for the educated and the scholarly? Can the ignorant, the heathen and the fool be saved? If so, it's got to be simple and basic.

For the past several years, our children have been exposed to so-called "new methods" of learning in the public school system. Recently, it has been noted that the basic reading, writing and arithmetic method was probably the best after all. As a result, new schools are now being built called "Back to Basics," and they're discovering that the students in these schools are far advanced over the others.

It's the same with the gospel. Traditional Christians are so hung up with sins and self-righteousness until they are miserable. They're sincere, but you can be sincerely wrong.

Now, once again, what is sin? Going any further without an answer to this age-old question would be useless. Without a Bible answer, we would still be like a ship without a rudder in trying to explain sin. The Bible must have the answer, and if it does we must let that be the final voice of authority ringing loud and clear. Does it have that answer? Yes, it does.

"Whosoever committeth sin transgresseth also the law: for sin is the transgression of the law." 1 John 3:4.

There is no way that you can get around this one. You can display your own little yardstick of holiness and exploit your private convictions, but when it comes to preaching "sin," here is your basic rule.

Understand this one thing: there is a difference in what is right and what is righteous, as well as what is sin and what is wrong. A thing can be wrong and not be a sin. This is what is so difficult for some people to accept. It's wrong to break a speed limit with your car, but it is not a sin. It's wrong to display bad manners, but not a sin. It's right to open a door for a lady, but there's nothing righteous about it.

But when you talk about the sin that breaks communion with God, you're talking about 1 John 3:4. To commit a sin, you must break a law. It is not difficult to determine the laws of God. You don't have to master the entire Word of God to know his commandments. It's not necessary to be a theologian or a Bible scholar. You can read four chapters from the Bible and know the commandments of God, and I'm going to prove it to you.

If anyone in the Bible was an authority on holy living, Christ would be the man. It was He who came that we might "have life and have it more abundantly." So, if anyone had the formula, Christ did.

Read, if you will, the Sermon on the Mount in Matthew, chapters 5-7. He covered it and covered it well. There has never been a more basic and authoritative message than that one. Christ gives the "dos" and the "don'ts." He lays the greatest and most thorough foundation for Christian living that could ever be laid.

What was the foundation for Christ's ministry? It was the fulfillment of the commandments found in Exodus 22. Christ never came to destroy the law. The biggest fault with the old commandments was in the fact that man couldn't keep them, and the reason that he couldn't keep them was that he had no salvation from sin. Sin was a part of his life. If he was sorry for his sins, the most that he could do about it was offer up a burnt sacrifice and ask forgiveness. God would then forgive him. But forgiveness of sins did not take them away. Sin in one's life is like having drugs in the bloodstream. As long as a trace of it is there, it will continue to crave for more. It's the same with sin.

A lady came to me one night during one of our revival campaigns. She was desperate and needed help.

She told me her problem. She had the habit of smoking and she really wanted deliverance. Before I prayed for her, I took the time to explain some basic facts to her. I told her that the reason her body craved for cigarettes was not solely due to a habit alone. I told her that her bloodstream was contaminated with the nicotine drug and as long as there was a trace of it there it would continue to crave for more and that what she had been doing was feeding that craving by smoking more.

When she realized that her dreaded craving would cease when her bloodstream was given time to cleanse itself, she then had the physical and mental strength to overcome.

Under the Old Testament law, man's sins were only temporarily forgiven until the next time. Jesus Christ had not yet come to the world. He would not only forgive sins, but His blood would wash them away completely.

So, it's easy to see the old prophets crying out so bitterly against sin. You might say that they even went as far as to preach fear into the people to turn from their wicked ways. There didn't seem to be any other or better way at the time.

This is not true for our day. We can live free from sin and its dominion, and it is not the difficult thing as it is sometimes preached to be.

SIN SEPARATES MEN FROM GOD

True sin, breaking the commandments of God

willfully, separates man from his relationship with God. But once again, let me emphasize that you cannot categorize every fault and failure to be sin. Here's a good explanation in Hebrews 12:1b: "...let us lay aside every weight and the sin which doth so easily beset us..."

Now this backs our former claim that certain things can be labeled as "wrong" and still not be a sin. Those things that are wrong can be termed as "weights" that deter our Christian lives and retard our spiritual growth. But this gives us no license to send people to hell because they have "weights" that we wish to label as "sins."

In Mark 10:17-22, Jesus was confronted with a question from a young man who asked, "Good Master, what shall I do that I may inherit eternal life?" He didn't ask what .he should do to live a good Christian life. He never asked what holy living was or what sin was, but what he would have to do to inherit eternal life.

Jesus proceeded to quote to him six of the Ten Commandments. I'm not certain as to why he stopped with these six. I have a feeling, according to the rest of the verse, that the young man interrupted him before He could finish assuring him that he had kept all of these commandments from his youth.

Think about this: that a man can inherit eternal life by simply keeping the commandments...*if* he can. But therein lays the big problem. Man cannot keep the commandments...until he is born again by the Spirit (John 3:3).

Now, once he is born again by the Spirit, is he then required to keep more commandments than he would otherwise? No. Now that he has been baptized into the body of Christ by the Holy Spirit, he has the power and the strength to keep the commandments, and he doesn't have to be a Philadelphia lawyer to understand what the commandments are. He doesn't have to have the entire Bible memorized either. The plan of salvation is a simple one. Christ died for our sins (not just because of our sins).

Now if sin is a transgression of the law and we know what the laws of God are, why should it be so complicated to understand what sin is?

ONLY TWO LAWS

As a matter of fact, Jesus revealed that the plan of salvation could be preached with only two commandments. Think about that. Only two! Now that would really ruin many church bylaws, wouldn't it? But hear what they were:

"Then one of them, which was a lawyer, asked him a question, tempting him, and saying, 'Master, which is the great commandment in the law?' Jesus said unto him, 'Thou shalt love the Lord thy God with all thy heart, and with all thy soul, and with all thy mind. This is the first and great commandment.'" (Matt. 22:35-38)

Now think about this for a moment. If a man really loved God that much, with all of his heart, soul, mind and strength, there would never be any worry about that man breaking any other commandment. Would there? That man would never lie, cheat or kill. He would never defraud his brother. He would never have other gods in his life. Why? Because he loves the Lord with all of his heart, soul and mind. How simple can you get?

But he hasn't finished yet. He has one more commandment to make this duet complete. Listen: "And the second is like unto it, Thou shalt love thy neighbour as thyself. On these two commandments hang all the law and the prophets." (vs. 39-40)

MISAPPROPRIATED EFFORTS

Our churches and ministers have spent their lives crying out against sin and felt that they were God's thundering prophets warning men and women of the pitfalls of life. We've been so protective of our children and taught them from our Sunday school classes about all of the things that they should and should not do to keep from losing their little souls in hell.

Ladies and gentlemen, the scriptures tell us that Jesus Christ came to this world that we might have LIFE (not gloom), and that we might have it more abundantly. And while protective ministers and over-protective parents spend their time teaching their children about how to wear their clothes, fix their faces and cut their hair, the real and genuine pitfalls of Satan are being laid for them for which they have not been prepared.

Holiness churches must be the worst of all when it comes to external righteousness. You see, the scriptures do not say, "Thou shalt not wear jewelry," but they do say "Thou shalt not commit adultery." It doesn't say, "Women shall not wear pants," but it does say, ''Thou shalt not bear false witness." Why is this so hard to understand?

What this boils down to is "private holiness yardsticks." Yes, you heard it right! Sure, everyone has their own "convictions," but let them remain as "personal convictions" and don't try to preach your convictions as sins to someone else.

Romans 14:14 says: "I know, and am persuaded by the Lord Jesus, that there is nothing unclean of itself: but to him that esteemeth any thing to be unclean, to him [not to someone else] it is unclean." Paul emphasized here that this revelation was not his, but that he received it from Jesus Christ.

YOU'VE COME A LONG WAY, BABY

Satan has literally made fools out of our churches and preachers. A few years ago we sent people to hell and turned them out of our churches because they attended the "moving picture shows." The things that they saw on the movie screens of their generation were like Mickey Mouse cartoons compared to what we are allowing to come into our living rooms today by way of television.

Externally, people were "dressed-up" for religion by wearing their dresses long, sleeves long, hair long and discarding their sinful jewelry and facial make-up. But the historical ledger revealed a side to the story that most of those old-timers hate to admit. These externalities did not thwart adultery when the occasion overcame them. It didn't discourage fighting and confusion on the church boards. It didn't keep the members from getting jealous of one another when one was given more duties or attention in the church than the other. It didn't keep them from excommunicating as many members as they took in. So, what did that have that was so great to brag about?

WE CAN'T TRANSFORM PEOPLE

Here we come right down to the bottom line. Our job is to preach the Gospel of Jesus Christ. We cannot reform people. Nor can we judge them. We can lead them to Calvary, but that is as far as we can go. It's up to the Lord from that point on. When that person leaves the feet of Jesus, they may not act the way you do, talk the way you do, see things the way you do, but unless they break a commandment of God, you have no right to judge them of evil. Keep your yardstick to yourself.

Paul said in 1 Corinthians 1:17: "For Christ sent me not to baptize but to preach the gospel..." Some people have a hard time accepting this scripture because of their hang-ups. You see, Paul was a basic preacher. He broke more traditional doctrines than any other man you've read of in the New Testament. He had difficulty convincing people that holy living was an experience from the heart and not something experienced in deed only.

Sometimes I wonder if people really have a clear concept of Jesus Christ and His true nature. "Watch out, the Lord will get you!" Is God really that way? Is He really a taskmaster with whip in hand, waiting to blister the first one who steps out of line? Is He a punishing God who gloats over the fact that you suffer from your sinful mistakes? Somebody has been preaching the wrong Jesus Christ! That is not the one in the scriptures.

"The Lord is merciful and gracious, slow to anger, and plenteous in mercy." (Psalms 103:8)

"The Lord is gracious, and full of compassion; slow to anger, and of great mercy. The Lord is good to all: and his tender mercies are over all his works." (Psalms 145:8-9)

"The Lord is...longsuffering to us-ward, not willing that any should perish, but that all should come to repentance." (2 Peter 3:9)

JUDGE NOT THAT YE BE NOT JUDGED

One Sunday morning I was preaching in this certain church and my subject was, "What does it mean to be born again?" I wasn't aware of the fact that the Sunday school lesson that morning was on the sin of adultery. Neither was I aware that the text I would use was also a part of the Sunday school lesson. Yes, you've guessed by now, I didn't go into the Sunday school class that morning. I suppose I was more interested in getting my mind ready for the morning message.

In any event, I took my text from the fourth chapter of John and preached about the woman who met Christ at the well. Now, I probably wouldn't have had too much of a problem with this congregation were it not for the fact that they were of a denomination who more or less preaches that "double marriage" is an unforgiveable and unpardonable sin.

"When a person is born again, his sins washed away, and he is born into the body of Christ," I said, "God wipes his slate clean and his life begins from that moment and God will never bring up his past to him again."

I noticed that the crowd, quite large, seemed to get a little restless on that one. But I didn't stop with that. I went on to use the woman at the well for my illustration. Her life had been the perfect example of sinful shambles. But she was a sinner. There was no way that she could change anything that she had done in the past, no matter how hard she tried. But she did do one thing right. She said: "Sir, give me this water, that I thirst not, neither come hither to draw." John 4:15.

She couldn't change her life, but she was now face to face with one who could change it. Five times she had been married to five separate men and presently she was living with a man who was not her husband. She could find it very simple to curtail her present love affair, but there was nothing that she could do about the five marriages that had ended in disaster.

The more that she talked to Jesus, the more she was convinced that this was more than a prophet to whom she was speaking. That conversation was enough to cause her to run to the city exclaiming, "Come, see a man, which told me all things that ever I did: is not this the Christ!" (John 4:29).

"I don't care if she had been married twenty-five times," I continued in that Sunday message. "When Christ forgives, He forgets, and when one is born again, his slate is wiped clean and his life starts all over again as though it never had a past." I was sure of my words and convinced through the anointing of the Spirit that this was it. This was the message for our day. God forgives and forgets, but people never forget anything.

Well, it was for certain that traditionalism would be my foe that Sunday morning, because the people were ready for me when I stepped down from the pulpit at the last "amen." They accused me of opening the door for "double-married" people to worship in church. I could hardly believe what I was hearing. It was the same old spirit that the prophet Jonah had when he learned of the goodness of God to forgive Nineveh. They would have preferred that I condemned these poor souls to everlasting torment than to tell them that twisted and perplexed lives are a result of sinful natures and that the "born again" experience in Jesus Christ could blot out their past and give them a new start.

The moment that the Samaritan woman surrendered her life to God, her past was wiped out. This is what "atonement" is. That God, through Christ Jesus, can so transform you until He would make you as though you have never sinned.

From that moment of commitment, her past faded away. As far as Christ was concerned, she had never been a sinner, never been an adulterer, never been married five times. She was now a new creation! Her life started from that moment.

If what I am saying now is not true, then the new birth is not really a new birth. Old things don't really pass away, as the Bible says, and all things don't become new.

What's wrong with us? Why can't we accept the Bible for what it says? Why do we have to be so hard, when God is so soft-hearted? Why must we be so unforgiving when God is so forgiving? Why must we be so unreasonable when God is so reasonable? What do we accomplish by being so complicated when the plan of salvation is so simple?

ADD ONS

You would be surprised to hear some of the things that I hear from people all over the country…their personal views of salvation and what a man should do to live a godly life.

What is the plan of salvation, anyway?

"For God sent not his Son into the world to condemn the world; but that the world through him might be saved." (John 3:17)

"That if thou shalt confess with thy mouth the Lord Jesus, and shalt believe in thine heart that God hath raised him from the dead, thou shalt be saved." (Romans 10:9)

"If we confess our sins, he is faithful and just to forgive us our sins, and to cleanse us from all unrighteousness." (1 John 1:9)

"For by one Spirit are we all baptized into one body." (1 Cor. 12:13)

But listen to the "holy saints:" "They weren't baptized right!" "They didn't stop doing the things that I quit doing!"

The scriptures say: "There is therefore NOW no condemnation to them which are in Christ Jesus, who walk not after the flesh, but after the Spirit." (Rom. 8:1)

Can you fathom this? Here are people who have just been born again, repented of their sins. They've been baptized by the Spirit, into the body of Jesus Christ. Yet people tell them that they aren't really saved until they do other things. This, my friend, is tacking on condemnation when the scriptures have told them that they were delivered from condemnation by virtue of being placed into the body of Christ.

Water baptism does not take away sin. External

reformations do not transform the heart. Verbal commitments do not purify the sinful soul.

Understand this one thing right now: I am not excusing sin nor paving the way for liberalism. But we speak of "rightly dividing the Word" but so rarely put it into practice. I'm against sin, but I want to be sure that what I am against is, indeed, sin.

WHO ARE WE PREACHING TO?

I preached a series of meetings one time for a certain denomination and they were critical of the fact that none of my sermons covered the sin of adultery. The conventions that I was addressing were composed mostly of church people. I couldn't understand why I should be preaching such subjects to sane, level-headed, Christian, church people who already knew that it was wrong to commit adultery. The very idea was absurd.

Even if my congregation had been totally sinners, what would I have gained if I did preach on the sin of adultery? What could I have accomplished if I had preached on the sin of taking drugs and drinking liquor? I could have told them, too, that it was a sin to steal and lie. And what would I have accomplished? I'll tell you. I would have insulted their intelligence. The Bible says that the unbeliever is condemned already in his heart (John 3:18).

Sinners know what kind of life they're living, and they know right from wrong. Christian people are supposed to know what evils exist, so why continue to remind them? They're not looking to hear something that they already know; they're looking for "a way out," a "way of escape." The world is looking for deliverance from condemnation and herein lays our reason for preaching faith, positive living and positive thinking.

You cannot teach a child until he is first born, and when he is born, he'll not learn everything about life his first day here.

The "Gospel" is "Good News!" It is not condemnation. It is not the old prophets' warning of doom. This is a new day. This is a day in which man can walk into the very presence of God and receive a personal audience with the Master. This is a day in which the shed blood of Jesus Christ can eliminate the core of sin in a man's life and start him out afresh and anew.

THE SECRET COMBINATION

Getting back to the basics of holy living now seems so simple, doesn't it? No longer wondering what sin is but knowing what sin is by simply knowing what God's commandments are. Breaking those commandments is committing sin. But who cares about breaking a commandment? If a man loves God with all of his heart, he doesn't desire to break God's commandments. He's in love with his Master.

Christ's coming into this world had a two-fold

purpose. He came as an eternal offering for our sins (John 18:37), and He came to lay the ultimate foundation for our holy lives (1 Cor. 3:11). You won't find the secret to holy living in the book of Revelation. You'll be strengthened in the faith when you read the book of Acts, but it is not the foundation of holy living. Where do you find it? Search the Word. No, I did not say to search the Bible, I said search the Word. John 1 tells us that the Word was Christ.

When you read the Gospels, you will find the Word. You'll read the greatest gospel material and hear the most outstanding gospel preaching and instruction that can be found anywhere in the world. Jesus, the author and finisher of our faith, gives us the details of sin and righteous living in his Sermon on the Mount from Matthew 5-7. He will tell you that. He didn't come to destroy the law (Matt. 5:17) but to make it possible for you to keep the law.

Think how simple this is. Knowing what sin is by knowing what the commandments are. But, who really cares anyway? I want to know what I can do to live a victorious life in Christ Jesus. If I can do that, I won't have to worry about sin because I am born again and sin no longer has dominion over me (Rom. 6:6).

Not only is it simple now to understand what sin is and how to live by simple commandments, but it is also simple to complete the real combination for holy living by adding the last verse of 1 Corinthians 13. Here are three things that will last through eternity: faith, hope and love. Faith can move mountains. Hope will strengthen you when the going gets rough. And love will keep you sweet and humble before the Lord when everything seems to go wrong.

Paul said that the greatest of these three was love. I believe him. It was a long time before I could really understand this. I didn't really understand the depth of this kind of love, but I have learned that this is the real jewel upon which every facet of your Christian experience revolves.

Paul spends a great deal of time and space with this thing called love by devoting the entire thirteenth chapter to it. When I read it, I understand more clearly why it is so important to let the love of God abound in your heart. Listen to a little of it:

"Though I speak with tongues...and have not love, I am a sounding brass...Though I have the gift of prophecy...understand all mysteries...have all knowledge...have all faith...remove mountains...and have not love, *I am nothing*...And though I...feed the poor ...give my body to be burned, and have not love, it profiteth me nothing."

But now, listen to what Paul says that the real love of God in a man would do:

"Love suffereth long…

...is kind...

...does not envy…

...doesn't boast...

...not puffed up...

...doesn't misbehave...
...doesn't seek to please itself...
...not easily provoked...
...thinks no evil...
...doesn't rejoice in iniquity...
...beareth all things...
...believeth all things...
...hopeth all things...
...endureth all things...
...never fails..."

What qualities! What character! Think about these for a moment. The love of God is shed abroad in our hearts by the Holy Ghost (Rom. 5:5). Real, genuine, God-given love is first longsuffering. This means that you will be slow to anger and will be merciful to those who may seem to be careless in their walk with God. You see, babes in Christ are not as strong as some of us, but the love of God will cause us to be patient with them.

"Love is kind." I like that. We could talk about the evils of sin until the Lord comes, but nothing can reach the heart of the sinner like love and kindness. These are the things that reveal Christ unto the world. What other way can you "let your light so shine before men that they may *see* your good works...""? Yes, He used the word, "works." Man is not saved by works, but it is for certain that "works" follow him.

Love will overlook people's faults and failures.

After all, all of us have made mistakes and someone had to look over ours. Yes, I have learned that true love in the Spirit is the greatest asset to a victorious Christian life.

ABUNDANT LIVING

Understand this one thing now: when we talk about getting back to basics, we're speaking of fundamental living, the foundation of a godly life. I don't mean to infer that this is all there is to living for God, but it is the secret of a godly life.

There are manifold benefits that automatically go along with your salvation experience that are the "extras," but they have nothing to do with salvation itself.

Healing is a part of your fringe benefits. But if you're sickly, it doesn't make you a sinner.

Water baptism and communion are religious acts of faith and dedication, but they have nothing to do with your eternal salvation.

The baptism in the Holy Spirit is the greatest gift that God ever gave to the born again believer, but it has nothing to do with your salvation.

It has become a very controversial subject as to whether one must be baptized in the Holy Ghost to enter heaven. If this doctrine were true, then it would mean that the blood of Jesus Christ and His death on the cross was not the real means of salvation. It would mean that we were saved by the infilling of the Holy

Ghost rather than our professing Jesus Christ as our Savior. It would mean that the Holy Ghost was not really a "gift" as mentioned in Acts 2:38, but an ultimate requirement for salvation.

I believe in all of these blessings from God, but I believe them to be just as the Bible teaches them: benefits of the King to the children of the Kingdom.

CUSTOMS ARE FOR PEOPLE, NOT GOD

Times change. There is no question about that. Church folks have preached for years that God doesn't change, and they're right about that. But as we have stated earlier, tradition is a slave-master that people themselves have created. Their ideologies are formed and they tend to place God's plan into that traditional mold. Then when people fail to conform to their way of thinking, they call it sin.

God's word doesn't require any translation. It's not that difficult to understand. Take it for what it says, it's just that simple.

Years ago, the church world considered a Pepsi cola or a Coke to be strong drink. God hasn't changed since then, but somebody wised up and saw how foolish they were. When I was a kid, it was wrong for a Christian woman to wear ankle socks. There was nothing in the commandments against wearing socks. On the other hand, there was nothing telling them that they could or should wear hosiery, but they did. God hasn't changed since then, but somebody has wised up.

THE BOTTOM LINE

"...for the Lord seeth not as man seeth; for man looketh on the outward appearance, but the Lord looketh on the heart." (1 Samuel 16:7)

We all have the same basic rules to follow. You don't have the time to stop and judge anyone else. You have no way of knowing their circumstances or the motives that lie in their hearts. You have no way of knowing what your actions or deeds would be should you face the same circumstances and conditions. Outside of breaking the commandments of God, there is no way for you to discern sin in anyone else's life. And even if you could, your declaring to them their sin would not give them deliverance. Remember, you overcome evil with good. And by the same thought, you overcome doubt with faith. You overcome the negative with the positive. You overcome a dull life by living a happy life.

Yes, the world will return to you what you give to it. Give it a smile. Give it happiness. Give it hope. Give it a reason to live. Give it peace of mind. Give it deliverance from fear. Give it deliverance from condemnation. Basically speaking...GIVE IT JESUS!

YOU CAN'T BLAME GOD

Some time back, a friend of mine, who incidentally was never one to place too much confidence in the significance of dreams, related a chilling story concerning a dream that he had, which in turn provoked this following sermon. He said:

"A few years ago, I was much disturbed about a dream that I had about seven o'clock in the morning. I had never been one to place any great significance in what I dreamed because more often than not my dreams were an after affect of my bad habit of eating too much before going to bed at night, but this was entirely different.

In this dream, I received a phone call from a mother in Arlington, Virginia concerning her son who had been killed in Vietnam. She and her family had never been regular church goers and so they had no pastor of their own.

In my dream, she asked if I would come to Arlington Virginia and preach her son's funeral and I consented.

Still in my dream, I remembered so vividly going to an army base were the funeral was to be conducted in a

74

military chapel. Most of the family, I recall, sat on the right side of the sanctuary facing the pulpit. There were a few military friends, however, who sat on the opposite side.

Somehow or other, I could hear voices and remarks coming from the side on which the family was seated. While the body of the young soldier lay in the casket, the family was questioning God as to why He had allowed this tragedy to happen.

The wife was pleading, "Why God, did you take my husband?" And the mother, "Why God did you take my youngest son?" Their voices and messages were so real.

While I sat listening to the voices of the mother, family and wife blaming God for this most unfortunate death, I thought of the more than 55,000 other young men who had met their untimely deaths from this brutal war. 55,000 other mothers, fathers and wives had probably questioned the Almighty God the same as these were doing.

At first, I didn't have the answers to their questions any more than any other minister or counselor. But suddenly, it all came to me. The reasoning was there, the scripture to support it was there. It was the answer and I would deliver it as my funeral message on that cold, rainy and miserable day.

After singing a song, "What a Day That Will Be" I walked slowly, but positively to the pulpit in an attempt to erase the questioning eyes that stared at me from the pews. I had the message and there were no doubts as far as I was concerned, that I also had the answers. Whether they would accept my message as a consoling and positive answer, I didn't know.

When my mouth came open, I said, "This morning, my message will be entitled "You Can't Blame God!" The countenance completely gave way to surprise on the faces of the audience. What kind of a statement is this? A young man has been killed and after all, everybody knows that "...the Lord giveth and the Lord taketh away," and why shouldn't we blame God?

But without giving way to any pause or misleading expression, I continued in my attempt to bury my case into the uncertain minds that protruded through the glaring, facial expressions.

My message began from the very beginning of the Bible. Perfection dominated the world and as far as God was concerned, it could and should have stayed that way forever. There was nothing to say that it had to change.

God had not purposed in his eternal blueprints that anything had to change. God delighted in the communion that he had with his man and woman. The animals and living creatures were a pleasure to him and he had no reason to wish it otherwise.

But what changed it? The Curse! Yes, the curse that was brought upon us as a result of that man and woman misusing their powers of choice and allowing sin to become a reality and opening the door for that sin to weave its way into the lives of millions, generation after generation to come.

The earth has a curse upon it that causes every existing thing to work contrary to the will of God. Whether it be sickness or war, it is contrary to the will of God and is a product of the curse.

In my dream, I had just finished the message while the Bible still remained open on the pulpit. At that point, someone was shaking me by the arm, saying, "Wake up, wake up, you've just received a phone call from Arlington, Virginia."

Rubbing my eyes and trying to get myself halfway awake, I learned that my wife had just received the message over the phone that a certain young boy had been killed in Vietnam and because neither he nor his family had a home church, they were asking me if I would preach the young man's funeral.,

Not yet completely awake, I told my wife, "That's alright, I know what to preach!" Then I turned back over in bed and went to sleep.

About an hour later I jumped out of bed when I realized what had taken place. I had just dreamed about something before it actually happened.

I wasn't a spiritualist, so I knew it had to be of God. I had to ask my wife once again to tell me if I had heard her correctly. She assured me that I had. At that point I was now even more intrigued to learn how much more of that dream would be a reality.

The following day, I saw the entire dream unfold

before my very eyes. The questioning mother and wife, the chapel on the base and it was all there just as I had dreamed it!

Realizing that my dream was of God, I proceeded to carry it out in every detail. Before I ministered to them, I sang the song, "What A Day That Will Be" and then announced my subject from the pulpit, "You Can't Blame God!"

THERE IS A REASON FOR ALL THINGS

Think for a moment of the many people whom you have known who have met with misfortunes in their lives and have placed the blame upon God.

Thousands of innocent children are born each year with birth defects and crippling diseases, and who gets the blame for it all? God!

When Pearl Harbor sparked the dreadful war with Japan and thousands lost their lives, who was blamed? God Almighty was blamed. Why can't He stop this war? Why did He allow it to happen?

Throughout the world, the terrible blows of international war have been felt. It has been felt through the chilling deterioration of the economy in leaning the paychecks and leaving many jobless.

The war areas have pictured thousands of starving children eating dirty, sloppy, waste food from the alley trash cans.

And how about the madmen like Adolf Hitler, Eichmann and Stalin who have made havoc of the world, and initiated some of the greatest holocausts that has ever been known to man?

Who takes the rap for the millions of Jews who were exterminated in the gas chambers of Germany and buried alive in mammoth graves? Almighty God has been accused as being responsible because they say that He allowed it to happen.

For many years now, dreaded diseases such as cancer, T.B. and heart disease has controlled the world's gross population status as a result of their toll on lives. They have presented themselves as uncontrollable monsters, walking around seeking whom they may devour.

They have had no mercy, stalking the young and the old alike, the rich and the poor. And who has been blamed for it all? God Almighty, because they say that He has allowed all of these diseases to happen for some reason that even they themselves do not understand.

Several years ago when more than 50,000 Latin Americans were smothered under an avalanche, resulting from a giant earthquake in less than one minute, the question rang around the world from the lips of so-called God-fearing people, "Why does God let these things happen?"

Eastern Africa recently has shaken the world with its appalling scenes of dead bodies stretched out on sun-baked grounds, having died cruel deaths for the lack of food and water. It seems natural that the human man must blame something or someone for all the misfortunes that cross his path. So, who is to blame for these starving creatures? "God is big enough to take it," they say, "let's blame God!"

The international scene is quickly reduced to home and the man next door or the one down the street and the one who works with you on the job, or a fellow Christian who attends the same church. To you they may be the mark of a perfect Christian. Their lives are spotless and uneventful from the evils of the world.

Then one day, all of their dedication to God and to their church appears helpless as they learn of being stricken with a terminal disease. "Why couldn't this have happened to someone else?" you ask. "Why did it have to happen to a saint of God? Doesn't God care anymore? Doesn't He have any feelings at all? Didn't He love them anymore? Doesn't He realize what this is doing to his image?"

At this point, we can think of all the degenerated people in the world that this could have happened to instead of one whose life is that of a saint. The scales of justice don't seem to balance out just right and we fall victims to blaming God.

Then while men and women all over the world are bringing unloved, unwanted healthy babies into the world, only to be unattended and abused while there are also those husbands and wives who spend ceaseless hours in prayer, hoping their home will soon be brightened by the birth of a child, only to be netted into a web of questions when a child is finally born...with terrible and heart-breaking defects. Whose fault is it when these things happen? Why God? Why did you let this happen to us? Why couldn't this have happened to one of those ungodly and careless parents? Why me?

"To everything there is a season, and a time to every purpose under heaven." (Eccl. 3:1) What a dynamic scripture revelation this is. But like all other scriptures in God's Holy Word, they are only as real to us as we believe them.

The Bible is a miracle within itself. Its promises can move mountains, part stormy waters, cleanse lepers, restore life, create and bring into existence. But it works only through one single turn of the combination: faith.

Believing in what the Word says and not just reading what it says. Therefore, if the Bible says there is a reason for all things, then there is a reason and we can find it if we search diligently.

THE BASIS OF A WARPED CREATION

First, where did sin come from? We can read the first few verses in the gospel of John which says, "All things were made by him; and without him was not anything made that was made (John 1:3), and conclude that God must have created sin himself. This doesn't sound logical but at least it's one point of view.

What is sin? Today, we see the results of it everywhere in almost anything. But where did it get started?

God knows for certain that it has made its reputation known throughout the world but where did it come from? What is its purpose and how did it get started?

If the Bible, God's Word, is the source of all truth, then it appears that it's the only place to find the answers that we're seeking.

It is found in 1 John 3:4. It says, "...for sin is the transgression of the law."

Now God couldn't have created sin because he is bound by nature to himself. He is law. How could he transgress himself?

Now, if God didn't create sin, then why did he allow sin? Well let's start all over.

God neither created sin nor a devil. In the very beginning, God created an anointed cherub and named him Lucifer (Ezek. 28:14) and he made himself a devil by using, or shall we say, abusing his power of choice.

The moment that Lucifer rebelled against God, he brought the act of sin into existence for the first time. Before this, only the possibility existed, not the very act or presence of sin. Sin is a transgression of the law.

From this, we can readily perceive your next question: "Why did God even create the possibility of sin? Why didn't God just create everybody holy and pure and just completely eliminate every possibility of sin whatsoever? Well, let's think about that for a moment.

First of all, why did God want humans to begin

with?

"…that they might be unto me for a people, and for a name, and for a praise, and for a GLORY…" (Jer. 13:11) Here it is in a nutshell. God created man to serve him. It would be a creation that would glorify him and one in which he could glory. Now, how could He glory from this creature if he was created with no power of choice? What father glories in a kiss or a hug around the neck from his child when they were forced into it? Doesn't make any sense, does it? It's only when that little boy or girl comes to you on their own and makes love to you that you glory from it.

Why do you serve God? Isn't it because you love him and you want to serve him? That's why He glories in your life. You go to church, not because you have to, but because you want to; and God is aware of this. If He gave you no power of choice, then He would be nothing more than a universal dictator, ruling from his throne on high with an iron rod and forcing you to serve him. What glory would He get from this? The only way that God could glory from man was through his own self-will to serve him.

So, sin came as a result of an "act" which Satan performed and ushered in a curse upon mankind.

THE RESULTS OF A WARPED CREATION

Some people have weird ideas about God and his work. Some really believe that He is a very busy weatherman sitting up there in his heavenly weather station pushing all kinds of weather buttons. They believe He pushes one button to make it snow in Alaska and another to make the sun shine in Miami, Florida. It's no wonder that people blame God for all of the natural disasters, they think He's either got his buttons crossed up or He's just being mean and hard to get along with.

The facts are that God has nothing to do with the when's and where's and the how's of weather. Now if this startles you a little, we may as well give you a few more startling facts that we're going to prove to you within the lids of this book:

1. God does not decide the cycles of weather anywhere in the world at any time.
2. God has nothing to do with the causes or continuation of wars anywhere throughout the world.
3. God has nothing to do with the diseases that are brought upon mankind.
4. God has nothing to do with the when's and the where's children are born or in what condition they are born.
5. God has nothing to do with the untimely deaths of either saints or sinner.

If these statements seem awkward to you, it is because you have overlooked the one missing link in the Bible that most other people have overlooked and this is your chance to piece the puzzle together.

When I was a child, I was like all other kids. I

asked the same age-old question that other kids ask their parents: "Where did I come from?"

Well, my mother and dad didn't want to give me that old "stork tale" so they just consoled me with the fact that "God made me and had an angel to bring me down from heaven." Of course a few years later they weren't so sure whose angel it was that brought me.

I believed that story until I grew up and learned different. From the pages of God's Word, I learned that God only created two people on this earth and that was my grandpa, Adam and my grandma, Eve. God created them...not me.

God, not only created them, but he created a "law" to go with them. It was the "law of reproduction." After He created them and gave them that law, He said, "Be fruitful, and multiply, and replenish the earth." (Gen. 1:29)

From that moment on, the law of reproduction has been in the hands of men. God set the whole system into operation and then turned it over to man.

It was the same with the rest of the creation. Nothing was created without laws to govern, whether it was beast, man or plant life. They all had one thing in common: governing laws.

What makes it rain? God speaking the word? God pushing a weather button in heaven? Or does God make the rain?

The laws of nature which He created determines the time and release of these natural elements. Why does it rain? It rains because the air contains moisture which has been collected through the drawing element of the sun and becomes visible as clouds, dew, etc. And when the temperature is cooled to a certain point, the visible moisture turns to droplets and it's time for you to put up your umbrella. Why does it rain? Because God created a law to take care of those things.

Should these rain droplets be forced upwardly to colder air and frozen, you will have hail and there are many variations of what could happen when you examine weather possibilities.

The weathermen have learned to forecast the weather because they know that when certain conditions meet certain conditions then certain results will take place. They have no hotline to God's throne for their information, they just rely upon those laws of nature, laws that God Almighty created in the beginning.

God created all things in the beginning, but He also created these laws to govern them. However, something happened. Everything worked perfect in the beginning. The creation was perfect and the laws that governed them worked perfect....and something happened to change all of this.

THE CURSE CAME

"For the Son of Man IS COME to seek and to save that which WAS LOST." (Luke 19:10)

This is not the general way that you hear this scripture quoted but this is the way the Bible records it.

You've probably heard it quoted most of the time as saying, "For the Son of man HAS COME to seek and to save that which IS LOST." But Christ didn't come to save that which "is" but that which "was" lost.

Everything that was perfect in the beginning was lost in the first few books of the Bible. Perfection was lost. Peace was lost. Perfect health was lost. A perfect creation was lost. Because of the sin (transgression of God's law) of Adam, the door was opened to blight the entire creation with a curse. Twigs would become thorns and the industrious insect would become a pestilent. Fun-loving animals would be turned into beasts and life-flowing germs would transform into ruthless disease carriers. Rivers would overflow their banks and mountains would tremble and move out of their places. Now the entire creation was blighted with a curse. Even the governing laws were warped and man crippled to the mercies of nature.

No sooner than Adam had become the doorway to that curse, he felt the results. A few minutes before, he was basking in glorious perfection with everything going his way. Now he is driven from the garden of paradise (Gen. 3:24) to earn his own keep by the sweat of his brow. Since that time, from that moment, nothing in the entire creation has been right. Everything has been wrong.

CAN GOD CHANGE THINGS?

God can do anything. There is no question about

this. But be assured that God has a way of doing things. It wasn't his fault that Lucifer turned himself into Satan. It wasn't his fault that Satan tempted Eve and Eve in turn tempted Adam. It wasn't God's fault that Adam forgot the commandment of God and yielded to temptation. God never has been at fault and has never wronged.

You must remember that the "warped laws" are contrary to God's will. And if this be true, which it is, then:

1. War and fighting are not God's will.
2. Natural calamities are not God's will.
3. Pestilences are not God's will.
4. Sickness and disease are not God's will.
5. Death is not God's will.
6. Disappointments are not God's will.
7. Poverty is not God's will.

And there are many, many other things we could name that are a direct result of the warped laws of nature which are contrary to God's will.

Once again we ask, "Can God do anything about any of this? Can He change things around? Can He make everything alright again? Or does He want to?"

Yes, God can and God wants to, but He is prevented. He stands beside the bed of that dying saint, plagued with a cancerous disease that has been a nightmare of pain and distress, desiring to stretch forth his hands to heal and make whole...but his hands are tied.

He looks from the portals of heaven and sees the starving millions in Africa and the Far East and his heart breaks over and over. He desires to feed the starving, cloth the naked and heal the sick...but his hands are tied.

He sees the bared windows of the prisons and mental institutions whose inmates have fallen victims to the warped laws of nature and he would like to "...set at liberty them that are bound..." (Luke 4:18) but He is prevented from doing so.

God is sick of war. The limp bodies of innocent soldiers doing their duty now lay in some swamp or rice paddy and the very sight of it brings a stink to the nostrils of God. If God had anything to do with it, it would have never happened. If God had anything to do with it, He would stop it. If God had anything to do with it, enemies would lay down their weapons of war, shake hands and live in peace. And God could do something about it, but his hands are tied.

And how about the man who just lost his job? What's he going to do about it? How is he going to support his family? Where is he to go when his landlord puts him out because he couldn't pay the rent? How is he to cope with the situation when his family is looking to him for answers and he has none? Isn't God concerned about this man? Does God have an answer for him and if so, why doesn't He move on his behalf?

Listen to me sir, it's time for this generation to come to grips with itself and realize why things are the way they are and that something can be done about it and blaming God is not the answer.

We have got to realize that God wants to stop war and bloodshed and that He wants to meet the special needs in our lives and that the warped laws of nature that have netted us into our depressive state is a curse that only Jesus Christ of Nazareth can break.

ONLY ONE ANSWER

I said that God has a way of doing things. Since man brought the curse upon himself, he must unlock the door that turns the tide.

Out of his own love, God made the first step by sending Jesus as a way out. This lets you know what He really meant when he said, "I am the way!" (John 14:6) Jesus can turn the tables in your direction. He can deliver the oppressed and heal the broken hearted. He can and He will because He is the way.

But, will He step over the boundaries of the warped laws of nature? Will He ignore the dividing lines and challenge the evil forces which turned against the creation in the beginning?

Once again, God wants to come to your rescue. God wants to set you free. He can and He will if, if, if... "If you'll only believe!"

This is the answer: ONLY BELIEVE!

Faith in God turns the tide and challenges the forces of nature. Faith will override the warped laws of nature and close the heavens that they rain not, open the Red Seas, lock the jaws of hungry lions, air condition fiery furnaces and raise the dead! This is all God is waiting for: someone to "touch the hem of his garment by faith." That's all.

The impossible then becomes possible. The unbelievable becomes a fact. The "never has been done before" becomes done.

That's God.

That's reality.

That's faith.

It is the simple key that has been overlooked. God can do what He really wants to do when someone calls upon him through faith.

His hands are untied through your faith. His hands are stretched out through your faith. He dispels the fears through your faith. He conquers devils through your faith. He performs supernatural miracles, only because you believed in him.

God wants your confidence. He wants your faith. Our God is happy only when He is doing what He likes to do best and that is making you happy. And this He can do only when you believe in him.

NOT THE WAY GOD WANTS IT

Sickness and poverty being God-inflicted is an age old fallacy. It existed in Christ's day. It was even evident in the oldest book of the Bible (the book of Job).

Nothing has changed since those days. People still cling to the way of least resistance. When they fail to understand something or fail to cure it, they immediately turn to put the blame on something or someone. Christian people are no exception; they do the same thing and it must break the heart of God.

Trying to justify themselves and their unbelief, they twist the Word of God into a pretzel and wring the scriptures out of context and force God into saying what He really didn't say at all.

They'll tell you that Job said, "…the Lord gave, and the Lord hath taken away." (Job 1:21)

But friends, everything in the Bible that you read isn't necessarily true. It depends on who is doing the talking. Remember there are a number of statements in the Bible that were made by Satan and Jesus call him the father of liars.

Have you heard people use the scripture, "an eye for an eye and a tooth for a tooth" to justify revenge? Yes, the Bible really says that...but have you ever read that scripture to see who was doing the talking?

"Ye have heard that it hath been said, an eye for an eye, and a tooth for a tooth, but I say [*Christ speaking*] unto you that ye resist not evil: but whosoever shall smite thee on thy right cheek, turn to him the other also." (Matthew 5:38-39)

So you can see that everything that you read in the Bible isn't true, only that which comes from the source of truth. This is the why Jesus encourages us to "Search the scriptures; for in them ye think ye have eternal life [*but which ones do?*] and they are they which testify of me." (John 5:39)

Now as for the statement which Job made, Job made it, not God. Job was a man who fell a victim to the warped laws of nature and took the easy way out by blaming his affliction upon God. Thus he says, "…the Lord gave, and the Lord hath taken away." His patience and endurance was to be admired but his knowledge of God's will was utterly incorrect.

In John 9, when the disciples saw a blind man who had been born in that condition, they immediately jumped to the wrong conclusion and asked the Lord, "Master, who did sin, this man, or his parents, that he was born blind?" (John 9:1)

This man had a birth defect which brought him into a sightless world. He could have been born without legs or arms just as easily. He could have been mentally retarded and the conclusions here would have been the same. Sure there was a reason, but the reason wasn't one that was due to God inflicting it because of some sin committed by either he or his parents.

It appears that Jesus answered this age old question once and for all in this passage, and yet people today ignore it completely and continue blindly with the same old fallacy.

"…but that the works of God should be made manifest in him" was the total answer that Jesus gave the inquiring disciples. It was simple. The man was a victim of the "warped laws of nature." God did not glory in the man's affliction, only in his deliverance. God glories out of delivering you and setting you free, not seeing you bound.

DON'T BLAME GOD...BELIEVE IN GOD

Some people react to kindness, some to flattery and others to various things, but God reacts to faith. When the leper said to Jesus, "...thou canst make me whole," it turned the embodied power of God on in Jesus and resulted in his pronouncing the leper made whole.

Failing to release that faith only prolongs your afflictions and irritating problems. The sickly woman of Matthew 9 continued to turn to the wrong source until she realized one day that the only source of help was Jesus.

Her pitiful cry couldn't touch him. Her disfigured face wasn't even noticed by him. Her frail body didn't move him. But the scriptures say, "For she said within herself, 'If I may but touch the hem of his garment, I shall be whole.'" (Matt. 9:21) To this, Jesus reacted. Her faith turned his abilities on. Her believing in him was too much for him to ignore. Faith moves God. Believing in him unties his hands to let him do his will in your life. "But Jesus turned about, and when He saw her he said, 'Daughter, be of good cheer; thy faith [*not her looks, not her money, not her pitiful cry, not her need, but her faith*] hath made thee whole.'"

"Fear not, little flock; for it is your Father's good pleasure to give you the kingdom." (Luke 12:32)

"The Lord taketh pleasure in them...that hope in his mercy." (Ps. 147:11)

"For the Lord taketh pleasure in his people: he will beautify the meek with salvation." (Ps. 149:4)

Don't blame God, believe in him. Turn your faith loose and he'll turn the world upside down to meet your needs.

God wants to move in your behalf more so than you want him to. This is God's pleasure. These are the things that God passes his time in: blessing and doing good things for his children. The warped laws of nature are contrary to God's will. Faith will cause God to intervene in the warped laws of nature and meet your need, however difficult.

Again we emphasize, don't blame God. Rather, believe in him.

PUT THE BLAME WHERE IT BELONGS

If God had anything to do with it, He would not allow thousands of children to be born in the poverty areas of the world when He knows their little lives will be a constant pain.

If God had anything to do with it, there would never have been a war.

If God had anything to do with it, there would never be a hospital or a grave.

If God had anything to do with it, there would never be a threatening cloud in the sky.

If God had anything to do with it there would never be a hungry stomach on the face of the earth.

But God didn't have anything to do with these things. They all are a result of the "warped laws of nature" due to the curse.

God can intervene. However, the key must be turned. The key that rebukes the winds and the rain; that casts out the controlling devils; that dries up the cancerous body; that restores the broken spirit is *faith in God.*

THE GIFT OF PENTECOST

Before his death, Christ taught his disciples the doctrine of the Holy Ghost Baptism. The following verse from the scriptures deal with this egregious subject.

"Nevertheless I tell you the truth; it is expedient for you that I go away: for if I go not away, the Comforter will not come unto you; but if I depart, I will send Him unto you." (John 16:7)

Notice that Christ said, "Nevertheless I tell you the truth." There are people today who will make you a promise and fail to keep it, but neighbor, when Jesus speaks, his words are Truth. You can depend upon his promises.

Christ spoke here of his departure and the disciples could not understand this. "The Son of Man shall be delivered into the hands of sinful men," Christ said, "and they shall slay Him, and the third day He shall rise again." His death they understood but to hear him say, "I will rise again," was far beyond them.

Christ was their teacher, leader and comforter. Now, they were saying, "Lord what shall we do when you are gone?" This signified their total dependency upon the Lord.

They couldn't bring their minds to the realization that Christ was leaving for He had said, "I must depart. It is to your advantage that I leave. For if I go not away the Comforter will not come unto you, but if I depart, I will send him unto you." My dear neighbor, Christ wants you and me to have this Holy Ghost baptism.

Now I realize that the devil may try to imitate this experience and has brought reproach upon it through the lives of certain people. Some will say I know Mr. So and So who claims to have this experience yet he doesn't live a true life. It's not everyone that speaks in tongues that truly has this experience with God. So, just because there may be one rotten apple in the basket doesn't mean that the rest of them aren't holding their true value. In other words, you cannot judge everyone by the life of one person.

Regardless of what you or anyone else may say, there is a genuine Holy Ghost baptism that God will give to them who will accept him. The Holy Ghost is a God-given gift.

Luke 11:11 says, "If a son shall ask bread of any of you that is a father, will he give him a stone? Or if he ask a fish, will he for a fish give a serpent? Or if he shall ask an egg, will he offer him a scorpion? If ye then, being evil, know how to give good gifts unto your children; how much more shall your heavenly Father give the Holy Spirit to them that ask Him?"

James 1:17 says, "Every good gift and every perfect gift is from above." The baptism that I am talking about is from above. Jesus said to the disciples, "...if I depart, I will send Him unto you."

There are some people today that teach that this experience was for the apostles only, but notice in Acts 2:39: "For the promise is unto you, and to your children, and to all that are afar off, even as many as the Lord your God shall call." Romans 13:1 says, "Let every soul be subject unto the Higher Power."

There are also others who believe that they received the Holy Ghost baptism at the time of their conversion. No, they did not, yet they did receive the Spirit of God.

Romans 8:9 says: "But ye are not in the flesh, but in the Spirit, if so be that the Spirit of God dwell in you. Now if any man have not the Spirit of Christ, he is none of his."

Romans 8:10: "And if Christ be in you, the body is dead because of sin; but the Spirit is life because of righteousness." Romans 8:11, "But if the Spirit of him that raised up Jesus from the dead dwell in you, He that raised up Christ from the dead shall also quicken you mortal bodies by His Spirit that dwelleth in you."

Romans 8:12 says: "Therefore, brethren we are debtors, not to the flesh, to live after the flesh, for if ye live after the flesh, ye shall die: but if ye through the Spirit do mortify the deeds of the body, ye shall live. For as many as are lead by the Spirit of God, they are the Sons of God. For ye have not received the spirit of bondage again to fear; but ye have received the Spirit of adoption, whereby we cry Abba, Father. The Spirit itself beareth witness with our spirit, that we are the children of God; and if children, then heirs; heirs of God, and joint-heirs with Christ; if so be that we suffer with him, that we may be also glorified together."

God's Holy Spirit is now here and you can receive him into your life. Remember that the Apostle Peter taught that this was a gift for you and to your children and even to as many as would be called into the realms of his redeeming arms.

It doesn't make any difference what church you may be affiliated with. The Holy Ghost is for all people of all faiths. This experience is not received by hypnosis or the sprinkling of powder on one's head as Pentecostals have been accused. If it was this simple there would be multitudes receiving him into their lives today. But no, there is a price to pay: the price of seeking God and dedicating your life to him. God's Spirit has fallen, so wade on out as it were an ocean and bathe your soul in its animated glory.

Acts 2:16-17 says: "But this is that which was spoken by the prophet Joel: 'And it shall come to pass in the last days' saith God, 'I will pour out my Spirit upon all flesh, and your sons and your daughters shall prophesy, and your young men shall see visions, and your old men shall dream dreams.'" This was the prophecy spoken by the prophet can be found in Joel

2:28-29.

Joel 2:23, "Be glad then ye children of Zion, and rejoice in the Lord your God: for He hath given you the former rain moderately, and He will cause to come down for you the rain, the former rain, and the latter rain in the first month."

This rain is falling today and I believe that is God's last day outpouring on the church. Regardless of what skeptics may say, may God help you to go forward in receiving this last day move of his Spirit.

WHO IS THE HOLY GHOST?

There are many people who cannot understand the necessity of receiving the Holy Ghost and neither do they comprehend the purpose of his work.

Until the Holy Ghost can make his abode in one's heart there will never be any power. People may run, shout and praise God, but until the Comforter makes his living quarters in their heart, they will never have the essential power to do service for God.

The Bible says, "But ye shall receive power, after that the Holy Ghost is come upon you: and ye shall be witnesses unto me both in Jerusalem, and in all Judaea, and in Samaria, and unto the uttermost part of the earth." (Acts 1:8)

There are many who have a Bible under their arm and who say they have a calling to preach. If you were to ask them if they have the experience of the Holy

Ghost baptism with the evidence of speaking with other tongues, do you know what they would say? "Why no, but I have been ordained by my church."

I do not believe you are qualified to preach just because your church has ordained you. Ordination is of no value unless it is of God. Those whom God calls He also qualifies. I believe that this Holy Spirit is He who ordains men and women to do the work of God.

Would Uncle Sam be so unwise as to give a man a gun and push him to the front lines without first training him? Men must be trained and given the necessary equipment before facing the enemy. God always equips his soldiers for his work on the field. Paul wrote, "Finally, my brethren, be strong in the Lord, and in the Power of His might. Put on the whole armor of God; that ye may be able to stand against the wiles of the devil. For we wrestle not against flesh and blood, but against principalities, against powers, against the rulers of the darkness of this world, against spiritual wickedness in high places. Wherefore take unto you the whole armor of God that ye may be able to withstand in the evil day, and having done all, to stand." (Eph. 6:10-13)

It is the desire of God that we be armored and I believe that the Holy Ghost is the most important part of our armor for it is He who gives us the authority to go forward in power.

I don't believe that any person should preach, teach a Sunday school class or serve in any capacity of the church without this experience. Jesus said that we would be witness unto Him "after" we received the Holy Ghost. Power would be at our command; power to tread on serpents and scorpions, and over all the power of the enemy without harm (see Luke 10:19). "And God wrought special miracles by the hands of Paul: so that from his body were brought unto the sick handkerchiefs or aprons, and the diseases departed from them." (Acts 19:11, 12)

"For to do whatsoever thy hand and thy counsel determined before to be done. And now Lord, behold their threatenings; and grant unto thy servants, that with all boldness they may speak thy word. By stretching forth thine hand to heal; and that signs and wonders may be done by the name of thy holy child Jesus. And when they had prayed, the place was shaken where they were assembled together; and they were all filled with the Holy Ghost, and they spake the word of God with boldness." (Acts 4:28-31)

"And these signs shall follow them that believe: in my name shall they cast out devils; they shall speak with new tongues; they shall take up serpents; and if they drink any deadly thing, it shall not hurt them; they shall lay hands on the sick, and they shall recover." (Mark 16:17, 18)

The Holy Ghost gives you the power to do all of these things and is your support in the hours of temptation. "When the enemy shall come in like a flood the Spirit of the Lord shall lift up a standard against him." (Isa. 59:19)

The Holy Ghost is the author of revivals. Many churches have tried time and time again to have revivals and have failed. They can't seem to understand why people won't come out to the services and why souls are not being saved. I believe that if the church would let the Holy Ghost work in his own way, churches would be filled and so would altars. God will move in our behalf if we, as the 120 people in Acts 2:1, will tarry until the answer comes from heaven.

Pentecost had fully come, over a week had past, then: "There came a sound from heaven as of a mighty rushing wind and it filled all the house where they were sitting. And there appeared unto them cloven tongues like as of fire, and it sat upon each of them. They were all filled with the Holy Ghost, and began to speak with other tongues, as the Spirit gave them utterance. When this was noised abroad, the multitude came together." (Acts 2:1-6) They didn't have to take pictures of Peter and run an ad in the papers or announce this revival on the radio. This revival announced itself. Today, if the church will seek God and let the Holy Ghost work, then they will see revival.

While in a revival in Pinnacle, North Carolina, the Lord told me that this was going to be a Holy Ghost revival. I failed to recognize the difference between a Holy Ghost revival and any other kind of revival. For three consecutive nights the Holy Ghost was the preacher. I did not need to beg people to make decisions. The gifts of the Spirit were manifested each night as they will always be in a Holy Ghost revival. This is the kind of revival that some people shy away from because it may reveal those hidden elements in their lives that show them up for less than the Christian saint they pretend to be.

Another great revival was in Samaria. "Then Philip went down to the city of Samaria, and preached Christ unto them. And the people with one accord gave heed unto those things which Philip spake, hearing and seeing the miracles which he did. For unclean spirits, crying with loud voice, came out of many that were possessed with them; and many taken with palsies, and that were lame, were healed. And there was great joy in that city." (Acts 8:5-8) Philip had no difficulty in having a revival in Samaria because the Holy Ghost was given full advantage.

No pastor will have any problem in having a revival if he follows the pattern of those just mentioned. Just get the church praying and seeking God. When the Holy Ghost begins to move He will be the principle evangelist. Again I say that the Holy Ghost is a revival sender. He is also a teacher, leader, and a comforter. "And I will pray the Father, and He shall give you another Comforter, that he may abide with you forever." (John 14:16) Verse 18 says, "I will not leave you comfortless; I will come to you." Verse 26 says, "But the Comforter, which is the Holy Ghost, whom the Father will send in my name, he shall teach you all things, and bring all things to your remembrance, whatsoever I have said unto you." "Howbeit when He, the Spirit of truth, is come, He will guide you into all truth: for He shall not speak of himself; but whatsoever He shall hear, that shall He speak: and He will shew you things to come." (John 16:13)

Without the Holy Ghost, we have no guide, leader or comforter. We need this experience for these perilous days of false teachers with their false doctrine that we may not err or stray from the right path.

The Holy Ghost is our medium of intercession with God. Paul says, "Likewise the Spirit also helpeth our infirmities: for we know not what we should pray for as we ought; but the Spirit itself maketh intercession for us with groanings which cannot be uttered." (Romans 8:26) Verse 27 says, "And he that searcheth the hearts knoweth what is the mind of the Spirit, because He maketh intercession for the saints according to the will of God."

Whenever we pray in the English language, the devil can understand what we are saying; but whenever the Holy Ghost prays to the Father through us, he becomes ignorant of what is being said. The saints have a private telephone line to heaven. There are no interrupted conversations for the Holy Ghost carries our message straight to the Father.

The scriptures which I have given you are enough proof of all the assets and blessings that this Holy

Ghost experience can provide to you. It is to your loss if you have not accepted this wonderful experience into your life. Now, it is left up to you as to whether or not you will go forward and take hold on this promised blessing.

THE ESSENTIALITY OF THE HOLY GHOST BAPTISM

People of today frequently ask why the Pentecostal people preach and talk so much about the Holy Ghost baptism. As we delve further into the written Word, it will tell us why it is so important.

First, the prophet says, "And it shall come to pass afterward, that I will pour out my Spirit upon all flesh; and your sons and your daughters shall prophesy; your old men shall dream dreams, your young men shall see visions; And also upon the servants and upon the handmaids in those days will I pour out my Spirit." (Joel 2:28, 29)

So important was the Pentecostal experience that Joel, the prophet, told about its forthcoming hundreds of years before Pentecost Day had "fully come." Can and does this prophesy stop here? Of course not. The prophesy is continued in the New Testament which records, "I indeed have baptized you with water; but He shall baptize you with the Holy Ghost." (Mark 1:8)

Again in Luke's writing we read, "John answered, saying unto them all, 'I indeed baptize you with water; but one mightier than I cometh, the latchet of whose shoes I am not worthy to unloose; He shall baptize you with the Holy Ghost and with fire.'" (Luke 3:16)

John the Baptist, the preacher of repentance, realized that there was a greater experience than that which he preached. John's gospel was the beginning of every Christian's life, but Christ's gospel would be the fullness of their life.

Christ has always been the example of his people. Herein lies the purpose of Christ himself receiving the Holy Ghost. "And Jesus, when He was baptized, went up straightway out of the water; and, lo, the heavens were opened unto him, and He saw the Spirit of God descending like a dove, and lighting upon him; And lo a voice from heaven, saying, 'This is my beloved Son, in whom I am well pleased.'" (Matt. 3:16, 17)

It is certain that if it was necessary for the Son of God to be filled with the Holy Spirit, it is much more needful for us today. No place in the Bible do you find that Christ was either tempted or had a victory over a temptation until after his endowment of power from above.

Though Christ was the Son of God, He was still subjected or exposed to failure. His divine personage did not exclude him from the fact that He too needed an inward power to thwart the evils of the world that He might stand.

After his experience He was led by the Spirit into the wilderness. Here, for forty days and nights He fasted and combated the temptations of Satan. Though tried by Satan himself, the Bible says, "And Jesus returned in the power of the Spirit into Galilee: and there went out a fame of Him through all the region round about. And He taught in their synagogues, being glorified of all." (Luke 4:14, 15)

DID CHRIST SPEAK WITH TONGUES?

I suppose you may deny that Christ ever spoke with other tongues. True, the scripture does not say He spoke with tongues at the time of his baptism, but does give evidence of it in other portions. Notice the following references:

Mark 7:34: "And looking up to heaven, He sighed, and saith unto him, 'Ephphatha,' that is, 'Be opened.'"

Mark 5:41: "And He took the damsel by the hand and said unto her, 'Talithacumi;' which is, being interpreted, 'Damsel, I say unto thee arise.'"

Notice especially that in each of these verses the Spirit gives the interpretation of what He said through Christ. Some say Christ was only speaking in his native tongue, the Aramaic language. The fact is that everything that Christ said in the New Testament He spoke in the Aramaic language, but it was not interpreted. Why were these few incidents interpreted? It was because these were the words of the Spirit unknown and unrecognizable by man. Matt. 27:46: "And about the ninth hour Jesus cried with a loud voice, saying, 'Eli, Eli, lama sabachthani?' That is to say, 'My God, my God, why hast thou forsaken me?'"

Many formal scholars say that Christ was only speaking here in His native tongue. If this be so, then why didn't the soldiers understand what He was saying? The Bible says they thought He was calling Elijah. "Eli, Eli" were the only words they understood. Eli, was a form of the word "Elijah" but was also a translated word for "God." But his discourse on the cross in its entire form had to be translated by the Spirit upon Matthew, the writer of this gospel, because these words that came from the lips of Christ were really coming from the Holy Ghost who was still living in his dying temple.

Jesus promoted the subject and made predictions concerning it for the future:

Acts 1:5: "For John truly baptized with water; but ye shall be baptized with the Holy Ghost not many days hence."

Luke 24:49: "And, behold, I send the promise of my Father upon you: but tarry ye in the city of Jerusalem, until ye be endued with power from on high."

Joel, John, Jesus and all of the apostles preached this experience. It is for certain that if we have this endowment, it will be our "assurance ticket" for the rapture.

"Then shall the kingdom of heaven be likened unto ten virgins, which took their, lamps, and went forth to meet the bridegroom. And five of them were wise, and five were foolish. They that were foolish took their lamps, and took no oil with them." (Matt.25:1-4)

Let me pause here for one moment. Here are ten virgins, five of them wise and five of them foolish. The five foolish virgins had lamps but failed to take the oil in their vessels with their lamps. The wise took oil both in their lamps (i.e. their experience with God) and in their vessels, (i.e. in their body; 1 Thess. 4:4) I believe this could represent the two sides of the church of our day. One side desires to seek God and receive the power of God into their lives, but the other side just wants a shallow experience. It's going to take the Holy Ghost power to go with Jesus when He comes, riding on the clouds of Glory for us to be able to go with him.

We wonder why God is moving across America today with a tidal wave of power, but this is God's way of saying, "prepare ye for the night hour is coming." I believe that before Jesus comes, there will come a "night hour" or an hour of persecution; a night hour period in which the cry will come.

In this parable, while the bridegroom tarried, the virgins slumbered and slept. Then at midnight the cry was made: "Behold, the bridegroom cometh; go ye out to meet him." They all arose and trimmed their lamps, but the foolish virgins had let their lamps go out while the wise had kept their lamps burning with the added supply which they carried in their vessels.

We may oftentimes be labeled as fanatics because we believe in wading out into the Spirit, but the testing time will come when the "non-fanatics" will be those who say, "Give us of your oil for our lamps are going out," and they shall hear the answer, "Not so, lest there be not enough for us and you."

First Peter 4:18: "And if the righteous scarcely be saved, where shall the ungodly and the sinner appear?"

The wise were the righteous who said goodbye to the world and were not found when the five foolish virgins returned after trying to buy a second rate experience somewhere. They knocked and pleaded but found the door shut in their faces.

The Bible says, "Let us therefore fear, lest a promise being left us of entering into his rest, any of you should seem to come short of it." (Heb. 4:1)

If one should hear the truth of the Holy Ghost and fail to seek for him, little chance there is for that person to successfully make the rapture. Don't look at the person who just got converted and ask, "What about them?" because God will take care of them if He has to fill them with the Spirit a split second before He appears. God is a merciful God.

That man or woman who has been sleeping on the altar for years will not make the rapture unless they get consecrated and receive the baptism. You say, "I'm seeking the Holy Ghost, what about me?" If there's an obstacle in your life serious enough to hinder your receiving the Holy Ghost, it may be serious enough to hinder your being quickened when Christ comes. Check and recheck your life and assure yourself of the reason why you haven't received this experience. It will mean everything to make it through.

"But if the Spirit of him that raised up Jesus from the dead dwell in you, He that raised Christ from the dead shall also quicken your mortal bodies by his Spirit that dwelleth in you." (Rom. 8:11)

When Christ appears and the resurrection dawns forth as a Morning Glory, you will see this same power, which aforetime you saw shake people's bodies and caused them to reel to and fro like drunk people, now change them from mortal to immortal and from corruption to incorruption. Realize now that you must have a quickening Spirit within you to be a part of that bride that will be caught away. Herein I have stated that you are going to need the Holy Ghost and even more so now that you have received enlightenment if it so be that you had not aforetime.

HOW TO RECEIVE THE HOLY GHOST

How may I receive the Holy Ghost?" Is this not the question asked by hundreds of inquiring seekers today? These are those who believe in the experience and have a desire for it but yet they are unable to yield themselves over to God to the extent that God will baptize them in the Spirit. The Bible says to walk in the light and He is the light. The advisable thing to do is to go before God and simply ask him to baptize you with and in the Holy Spirit and receive the Holy Ghost into your life.

WHEN THE HOLY GHOST FIRST CAME

"And behold, I send the promise of my Father upon you; but tarry ye in the city of Jerusalem until ye be endued with power from on high." (Luke 24:49)

So then about 120 people prepared themselves and went to the upper room to fill Christ's commission to them. The small number of Christians going to this room to tarry is worth giving attention to here. All you have to do is thumb the pages of God's Word backward a few chapters and you see 4,000 people listening to Christ's teaching and eating of bread broken by his hands. A few more pages backward and there is another multitude of 5,000 also eating from the Lord's hand. But where is the multitude now? Only 120 are going to tarry. Only a handful is willing to sacrifice for the blessing.

The big hindrance for many people is not that they don't know how to receive the baptism but just don't want to get right down to business with God. They are always ready to eat or to listen but never to put forth any effort on their own to receive the blessing.

One hundred and twenty saints are now waiting, praying, desiring, expecting and tarrying for the promised gift from above. By the end of one full week, something happened.

"And when the day of Pentecost was fully come, they were all with one accord in one place. And suddenly there came a sound from heaven as of a rushing mighty wind, and it filled all the house where they were sitting. And there appeared unto them cloven tongues like as of fire, and it sat upon each of them. And they were all filled with the Holy Ghost and began to speak with other tongues as the Spirit gave them utterance." (Acts 2:1-4)

The Holy Ghost fell. Now Christ had kept his promise to them. The disciples knew that their leader had made it back to his Father and had sent the promised gift.

THE HOLY GHOST IN THIS DAY

We talk a great deal about seeking for the Holy Ghost. But did you know that there is not one scripture in the Bible that teaches that men tarried for this experience after the Day of Pentecost had fully come? A power that has already fallen need not be sought for again. The 120 did the tarrying. We simply receive that which has already come. However, people have to pray to prepare themselves for the Holy Ghost to come into their lives.

Many today are asking God to fill them with the Holy Spirit when both they and God know that their heart isn't ready for such an experience. The Holy Spirit cannot and will not come in where doubt, fear or sin dwells. That heart must be clean and have faith. In biblical terminology, you must be sanctified. "I pray not that thou shouldest take them out of the world, but that thou shouldest keep them from evil. They are not of the world, even as I am not of the world. Sanctify them through thy truth; thy word is truth." (John 17:15-17)

"Wherefore Jesus also, that He might sanctify the people with his own blood, suffered without the gate." (Heb. 13:12)

"Jude, the servant of Jesus Christ, and brother of James, to them that are sanctified by God the Father, and preserved in Jesus Christ and called..." (Jude 1:1)

"And Joshua said unto the people, 'Sanctify yourselves; for tomorrow the Lord will do wonders among you.'" (Joshua 3:5)

Joshua's implication to these people was to clean themselves up, purify and make holy, that God may be able to perform wonders before them. This is God's command for the world today. God will send power and wonders but people must first separate themselves from carnality.

Various accounts are given in the Bible of those who received the Holy Ghost and how they received him.

"...who, when they were come down, prayed for them, that they might receive the Holy Ghost."

"Prayed for" here doesn't say for how long. I believe that these apostles were getting them ready for this experience they were desirous of. "...then laid they their hands on them, and they received the Holy Ghost." (Acts 8:15-17)

"And Ananias went his way, and entered into the

house; and putting his hands on him said, 'Brother Saul, the Lord, even Jesus, that appeared unto thee in the way, as thou earnest, hath sent me, that thou mightest receive thy sight, and be filled with the Holy Ghost.'" (Acts 9:17)

Acts 19 gives an account of Paul's visit to Ephesus where he found some men there who had not yet received the Holy Ghost. So Paul said, "Have ye received the Holy Ghost since ye believed?" They replied, "We haven't even heard whether there be any Holy Ghost." Paul said unto them, "Unto what then were ye baptized?" And they said, "Unto John's baptism. Then Paul exhorted them. And then he laid hands on them and they received the Holy Ghost and spake in tongues.

In my personal ministry I have seen many receive this experience in this fashion. When that anointed hand is laid upon you it will depend on whether or not you are ready. God is always ready.

"While Peter yet spake these words the Holy Ghost fell on all them which heard the word. And they of the circumcision which believed were astonished, as many came with Peter, because that on the Gentiles also was poured out the gift of the Holy Ghost. For they heard them speak with tongues, and magnify God. Then answered Peter, 'Can any man forbid water, that these should not be baptized, which have received the Holy Ghost as well as we?' And he commanded them to be baptized in the name of the Lord. Then prayed they him to tarry certain days."

Notice that while Peter yet spake that the Holy Ghost fell on them. I believe that God will do the same today if people will prepare themselves.

You don't have to be kneeling in church but you can be in the bedroom of your home, riding down the highway in your automobile, being baptized in water or anywhere. The Bible gives no demands of posture or place, only the condition of the heart. Yet, there are many good people who are holy and upright who cannot receive the Pentecostal baptism. This is probably due to the fact that they're just ignorant of how to yield themselves to the Spirit. The scripture says: "He that believeth on me, as the scripture hath said, out of his belly shall flow rivers of living water. But this spake He of the Spirit, which they that believe on him should receive: For the Holy Ghost was not yet given, because that Jesus was not yet glorified." (John 7:38, 39)

Some think the Holy Ghost comes into the head first and then to the heart. "Out of the abundance of your heart the mouth speaketh," the Bible says. "Out of your belly shall flow rivers of living water."

I am reminded at this point concerning an experience I encountered in one revival meeting. A young man had been seeking God for several nights for the Holy Ghost. The power of the Spirit would slay him and he would fall prostrate on the floor; his body would tremble under the power and yet he could never receive the Holy Ghost. Finally I asked him if he ever felt foreign words try to form on the inside while under the influence of the Spirit. He said he had. I encouraged him then to let those words go out of him for they were stammering lips of the Spirit trying to speak the Holy Ghost language. The next time he obeyed and God baptized him with the Pentecostal blessing.

You will never receive the Holy Ghost by speaking in other tongues, but by believing. The Holy Ghost comes in first from the heart. When you feel your lips quiver and your body chilled with waves of glory you are experiencing the Holy Ghost coming into your temple. He's there, but cannot stay or even speak until you believe that He is there. After you believe, then He will speak.

A man told me once that he was 66 years old and had been seeking the Lord since 1937. But I knew better, for if he had been seeking the Lord that long he would be a power house for God.

I asked him if he would like to die never experiencing the joy of the Holy Ghost. He then got down to business and received the Holy Ghost. Afterward he rejoiced as to how easy it was for him to receive the experience after he had been enlightened.

The Holy Ghost is a gift. If I hand you ten dollars and tell you that it is a gift for you, would you sit there and just look at me? Of course not. You would stretch out your hand and take it. But, if I say that you must work for it, it is no longer a gift but a wage. You need not work for the Holy Ghost for God is handing it to you with outstretched hands. Now, you stretch out your hand and take it. It is God's gift to you

WHO SPEAKS WITH OTHER TONGUES?

For years there has been great contention in nominal churches concerning the doctrine of tongues. However, we are compelled to consult the Word of God before we are able to draw any conclusive lines. Let us see if we can determine why so many read 1 Cor. 14 and say that Paul, the apostle, preached against tongues.

"Follow after charity, and desire Spiritual gifts, but rather that ye may prophesy. For he that speaketh in an unknown tongue speaketh not unto men but unto God; for no man understandeth him; howbeit in the Spirit he speaketh mysteries." (1 Cor. 14:1, 2)

Now I wonder, for those who refute tongues completely, what do you do with these scriptures? And you who believe that there must be an interpretation for every tongue?

Paul said that at this time when we speak we are speaking to God. A time when even the devil doesn't understand what we are asking God for, for the Spirit makes intercession for the soul.

Notice that Paul's letter was written to a young church that didn't understand the working of the Spirit. "Now brethren, if I come unto you speaking with tongues, what shall I profit you, except I speak to you either by revelation, or by knowledge, or by prophesying, or by doctrine," (vs. 6) In other words, Paul said it would be unprofitable to the church if he came preaching in tongues.

He also said that if you were having church and all spoke with tongues and there are those who occupy the room of the unlearned, they would say you were mad. He says that when one speaks in tongues let him pray that he may interpret, but if there be no interpretation, let him keep silent and speak to himself.

But this was not so with the Corinthians. When they prayed, they prayed in tongues; when they sang they sang in tongues. Paul said, "I will pray with the Spirit, and I will pray with the understanding also; I will sing with the Spirit, and I will sing with the understanding also."

First Cor. 14:19 is a favorite scripture for the opposing heckler, "Yet in the church I had rather speak five words with my understanding, that by my voice I might teach others also, than ten thousand words in an unknown tongue." But may I ask you where was Paul speaking about? He said in the church for the purpose of teaching others.

You cannot stop here. It would be detrimental both to you and this subject if we stopped here. Or do you want to stop here rather than read verse 18? Paul said here, "I thank my God I speak with tongues more than ye all."

Many say today that Paul is their preacher, but if

Paul is your preacher why don't you get the Holy Ghost like he taught it? Paul was not forbidding the speaking of tongues but teaching how tongues were to be used.

I believe that you will speak in tongues when you receive the Holy Ghost. When He comes He will come talking and speaking for himself.

"And they were all filled with the Holy Ghost and began to speak with other tongues, as the Spirit gave them utterance. And there were dwelling at Jerusalem Jews, devout men, out of every nation under heaven. Now when this was noised abroad, the multitude came together, and were confounded, because that every man heard them speak in his own language. And they were all amazed and marveled, saying one to another, 'Behold, are not all these which speak Galileans? And how hear we every man in our own tongue, wherein we were born?'" (Acts 2:4-8)

So you see 120 people received this marvelous experience and the Bible says they all spoke with tongues.

The amazing thing that convinced the multitude was the fact that they were composed of seventeen nations and dialects. But when Peter stood up to preach they were all able to understand him. This was a feat for more than what ordinary Galilean fisherman could perform. This was the convincing strategy of the Holy Ghost. When Peter's sermon concluded they cried, "Men and brethren what shall we do?"

Peter went to Cornelius' house and when Peter

arrived, Cornelius said, "We are all here present before God, to hear all things that are commanded thee of God."

"Then Peter began to preach, and while Peter yet spoke these words the Holy Ghost fell on all them which heard the word. And they of the circumcision which believed were astonished, as many as came with Peter, because that on the Gentiles also was poured out the gift of the Holy Ghost. For they heard them speak with tongues, and magnify God." (Acts 10:44-46) Here the Holy Ghost was poured out upon the Gentiles and they too spoke with other tongues.

In Acts 19, Paul came to Ephesus and found some who had not been baptized in the Holy Ghost. After he had explained the experience unto them he laid his hands upon them, the Holy Ghost came on them; and they spoke with tongues and prophesied. (vs. 6)

Here, as well as other places mentioned, the Bible says they received the Holy Ghost talking with tongues. I challenge any man or woman who says you don't speak in other tongues when you receive the Holy Ghost. If you don't speak with tongues, you don't have the baptism. This is your only medium of knowing for yourself that you have the experience.

There may be some who believe that you must have the gift of tongues to speak in tongues. This is not so. There is a difference in "speaking in tongues," which is the evidence of your experience, and the "gift of tongues," which not all have.

I charge you to close your eyes and ears to these preachers and teachers who oppose "tongues." Many of these will be lost because they failed to obey God's Word. Some may be like Saul of Tarsus, but very few. Go forward for God and do not stop until you have received the Holy Ghost with the evidence of speaking in other tongues. It is for you.

"For the promise is unto you, and to your children, and to all that are afar off, even as many as the Lord our God shall call." (Acts 2:39)

Now let me warn you, after you have received this experience, many of your close friends may make fun of you. It will be in times such as these that you will need the Holy Ghost to help you stand and face the mocking of the skeptics. After you have experienced this gift, you can say with me that all who receive the Holy Ghost do and will speak with tongues.

All the devils in hell or out of hell cannot make me doubt what I have written because I know whereof I speak.

In the last few months of my ministry, I have seen a great number of souls receive the baptism. Every one of them spoke in tongues when they received this gift of God.

Oh, neighbor, don't sit idle. Go forward for God for there is no time for you to be slack. Now is the time for work and work until you have discovered this experience which I have written about. May God bless you as you seek Him for a deeper experience.

A CONCLUSIVE THOUGHT

What I have written has been from my heart with a passion of love for those who sit in darkness. Many in this eccentric era don't have a leader who will preach this experience and teach the working power of the Holy Ghost.

The reason for this may be that many of them have sins in their life or something hid that would be revealed if the power of God began to fall. It may be also that they are envious as were the Pharisees. They don't have the experience and don't want anyone else to have it.

Regardless of what your pastor or teacher may say, you must seek God for yourself. They're not going either to heaven or hell for you; they will not stand in judgment for you but you will stand for yourself.

As has been stated earlier, the Holy Ghost is an important part of a Christian life. With him one can live a more dedicated life and do so much more for God.

"And when He is come, He will reprove the world of sin, and of righteousness, and of judgment: Of sin, because they believe not on me. Of righteousness, because I go to my Father, and ye see me no more. Of judgment, because the prince of this world is judged." (John 16:8-11)

All this the Holy Ghost does for the child of God. Now you can understand why I feel so strongly the necessity of this experience. With him you are able to stand against the evil forces of hell and live a victorious life for Christ.

I know whereof I speak because about eleven years ago the Holy Ghost came into my life witnessing with other tongues. I thank God for this marvelous experience and if God can do this for me, He can do the same for you also. Paul gives an absolute charge: "And be ye not drunk with wine, wherein is excess; but be filled with the Spirit." (Eph. 5:18)

Let me encourage you to continue seeking God earnestly and receive the promised gift which God gives to them that obey. I close, praying, that everyone who reads this and hasn't received the Pentecostal blessing, will receive it with joy.

AN ANALYSIS OF THE SPIRIT

Perhaps one of the greatest downfalls of man is his taking simple things in life for granted. And yet those things termed as "simple" turn out to be the keys to life and prosperity. Water and air are simple elements that the human takes for granted but couldn't live without. How easy it is to accept the fact that they are with us, always will be, not necessarily to talk about or to think about. Yet life doesn't exist without them.

The shame of it all is that those things which we take for granted are the things which we either have in abundance or have accepted as a way of life.

Now think about these two ideas: *Abundance* and a *Way of Life*. What are those things which we have in an abundant measure? Religion, churches, preachers, teachers, Bibles, religious schools, revivals, Sunday Schools and many more similar things that have to do with our religious heritage here in America. So, it's easy to see why our religion, whatever it may be, has been so easy to take for granted.

Denominationalism has been accepted as a way of life. Each with their own following have fallen into their own individual traditional patterns. Their doctrines follow more along the line of forefather interpretation of the scriptures, much more so that the actual scriptures themselves. The old died-in-the-wool attitudes of these people to continue in what they have always heard preached is the reason that most Baptists will always be Baptist and Methodists continue being Methodist, etc.

This kind of thinking is the real and genuine revelation of Christ's "blind leaders of the blind" story. It is a dangerous road to fall victim to. The "pride of life" weaves the web of deception and the "father like son" road is paved. God's Word and it's all important truths take a back seat to tradition as generation after generation follow the paths of what they have been taught all of their lives in that particular church organization. After all, what is it that separates denominations? Isn't it their differences of interpreting the scriptures? Common sense, let alone pure knowledge, will tell you that everybody can't be right and there's got to be some sensible reason why the scriptures cannot be settled upon once and for all.

The carnal mind cannot accept certain divine truths of the scriptures for they are conflicting with his nature (see Rom. 8:7). Thus, he sets out to pretend that he's a believer in the scriptures for appearance and conscience sake, but still he'll interpret them to his own satisfaction. As you would assume, this indicates that "everyone who saith Lord, Lord" is not of God, regardless of how high up the social ladder they are in their denominational circles. First Corinthians 1 bears this out. The old attitude of "I am of Paul and I of Cephas" brought division in the religious world that has never been abolished. Of course, Paul put them to silence in their belief that there were any differences in his doctrine and that of Cephas, Apollos and Christ. The differences existed among them because of their willingness or unwillingness to accept the whole truth. "Is Christ divided?" was Paul's question.

Thus, the differences of interpreting the scriptures today are not in the fact that God is using the same Word to say different things to different people, but in the fact that the church world has been so infiltrated with carnal and worldly minds, whose mouths are professing one thing while their hearts feel another.

Such are the obstacles that this chapter will be confronting in studying the Spirit-filled life.

If it were possible that you could now erase from your mind all of the details and beliefs concerning the "Spirit" that you have been taught or have believed all of your life because of those things which you have heard (especially those questionable things that you could never fully understand), then I believe we can open up a new dimension in your Christian life. It seemed you could never get all the puzzle pieces to fit in place but you accepted it as truth because of what you had been taught.

Here, for an example, are some of the questions

that we are about to answer with biblical record, so as to give you the opportunity to put all the pieces of the puzzle together and give you peace of mind.

1. What is the manifestation of the Spirit?
2. What are "the gifts"?
3. What is the difference between "faith" and "the gift of faith"?
4. What are "tongues"?
5. What is "the gift of tongues"?
6. What is "the unknown tongue"?
7. What is the "gift of the word of knowledge"?
8. What is the evidence of a Spirit-filled life?
9. What is "The Holy Spirit?"

WHO/WHAT IS THE SPIRIT?

The word, "spirit" is rendered in the Hebrew "ruach" 237 times and the Greek, "pneuma" 385 times. The primary meaning of both languages is "an invisible force" which is probably a far better rendition than most of the modern translations of today. The "invisible force" of a man is his will, intellect, conscience, etc.

In the Bible, the word, "Spirit" is used as:
- God's personal spirit - Ps. 139:7 Isa. 30:1 Isa. 40:13
- Holy Spirit - Gen. 1:2 Isa. 48:16 Zech. 12:10
- Angels - Ps. 104:4 Heb. 1:7
- Devils - Lev. 19:31

- Converted nature -1 Cor. 6:17
- Man spirit -1 Cor. 2:11
- Nature of the world -1 Cor. 2:12
- Wind - Eze. 37:9

The term, "Holy Spirit" is rendered synonymous to "The Holy Ghost" throughout the scriptures and we shall refer to both placed in man by God.

While Jesus Christ walked upon this earth He was the "force" that defied the laws of nature by healing the sick, raising the dead, multiplying the food supply, calming the storms and the solving of the problems of men. There was nothing impossible for him to do (see Matt. 19:26).

"And it came to pass in those days that Jesus came from Nazareth of Galilee, and was baptized of John in Jordan. And straightway coming up out of the water, He saw the heavens opened, and the Spirit like a dove descending upon him: And there came a voice from heaven, saying, 'Thou art my beloved Son, in whom I am well pleased.' And immediately the spirit driveth him into the wilderness." (Mark 1:9-12)

Notice that twelfth verse, "the spirit driveth him." The Holy Spirit is that "invisible force" when indwelled in the body and soul of a man that causes him to become "a visible force" for the kingdom of God. This we do know, that the Holy Ghost has no limitations as to his ability.

Jesus Christ of Nazareth was the coveted image of

man. He possessed every quality and attribute that any man could ask for. This is why such multitudes followed him and caused the disciples to exclaim, "All men seek for thee!" What was it that men saw in Him that was so magnetic, in such magnitude?

WHAT MEN SAW IN CHRIST

1. Perfection - Isa. 53:9; John 18:38
2. Unwavering nerve - Mark 4:41
3. Answers - John 7:46
4. Gift of knowledge - Mark 2:8; Luke 5:22
5. Gift of wisdom and understanding - Matt. 13:54; Luke 2:40
6. Gift of healing - Matt. 8:16
7. Gift of miracles - Matt. 21:19; Mark 6:38-43; Matt. 17:27
8. Gift of prophecy - Matt. 24; Luke 21
9. Gift of faith - Matt. 6:30; Luke 17:5
10. Endless resources - Mark 6:38; Matt. 17:27

Seeing the attributes that Christ possessed, men would follow him anywhere without any regard to the situation, place or circumstance. They gained strength from him psychologically as well as spiritually. Paul mentions that the strong should bear the infirmities of the weak (Rom. 15:1) and this was what was happening in the life of Christ. People who are weak, whether in ability, spirit or mind, often like to be in the company of strong-minded, strong-willed people, because it makes them feel stronger and more secure. The magnitude of Christ's attraction is seen in Mark 8:1-3: "In those days the multitude being very great, and having nothing to eat, Jesus called his disciples unto him, and saith unto them, 'I have compassion on the multitude, because they have now been with me three days, and have nothing to eat: And if I send them away fasting to their own houses, they will faint by the way: for divers of them came from far.'"

Distance from home did not matter nor did the fact that they had not eaten for three days. They only wanted to be with Jesus, where He was, see what He did, hear what He had to say, draw strength from his strength. Jesus Christ, what a man.

THE "IMAGE" ANNOUNCES HIS END

How do you break such news to loyal followers? These were men who had forsaken jobs, families and homes to be taught under his teaching. The things which they had seen and heard of him during the past three years had changed their lives, their thinking and their concept of serving God. There was no question as to how they would feel if Christ told them that He was leaving.

In order to break the news to them gently and yet leave them with a divine assurance that everything would be alright, He opened his startling remarks with "Let not your heart be troubled: ye believe In God, believe also in me." (John 14:1) This was the best way to prepare them for the latter statement, "I go to prepare a place for you, I will come again, and receive you unto myself; that where I am, there ye may be also."

Nothing was asked as to when He was going, only to when He was coming back. Nothing was asked of Christ concerning the mansions in the Father's house or what was there or where it was. They only wanted to know when He was coming back. What dedication! They only wanted to be with the Master and to think of their association coming to an end was disheartening and discouraging. It brought sorrow. Their source of strength was leaving them. They had leaned upon him for security, for peace of mind, for answers, for solutions to their problems. This meant to them that when Christ left all of these blessings would leave with him.

I WILL NOT LEAVE YOU COMFORTLESS

How do you get across to carnal minds that life can go on with the same force, power and productivity without the visible person of Christ? "If you love me, keep my commandments." In other words, Christ was saying, "If you ever believed in me at all, then you must believe in me now. If you believe in me when you can see me, then you must believe in me when you can't see me." There's only one combination that can bridge the chasm between the disciples and the invisible Christ and that is to keep his commandments. Something happens when men and women keep the commandments of Christ whether or not they can see him, hear him or touch him. Christ said, "If you love me, keep my commandments. And I will pray the Father, and He shall give you another Comforter, that He may abide with you forever." This is what Christ had been to them, a comforter. He was there when they were oppressed by the Roman aliens. He was there when they were sick. He was there when they were without. He was there when problems mounted and no answers could be found. Christ was their comforter. But now He says, "I will not leave you comfortless." (John 14:18)

The finite minds of such earthly creatures were incapable of fathoming the depths of such a divine truth that there could be a "Spirit" instilled in them which could give them the same comfort, the same answers and the same power that they had drawn from that man from Galilee.

For four chapters Jesus Christ (the Way, the Truth and the Life) gave them promise after promise that could only bring comfort to the dismayed hearts. He pledged that the Comforter whom the Father would send unto them would "abide with you forever." (John 14:16) This was a prophecy which John the Baptist had made (Luke 3:16) and was yet to be fulfilled. It was evident that the prophecy was yet to be fulfilled according to the way the scripture reads: "Howbeit when He, the Spirit of Truth, is come He will guide you into all truth..." (John 16:13). "When He is come" indicates a future event. It is also mentioned in the eighth verse of the same chapter in the same manner. "And when He is come, He will reprove the world of sin..." One thing is for certain – when He, the Spirit, came He would reprove (John 16:8), would guide (vs. 13), would glorify Jesus (vs. 14), would be man's source of power (John 14:12 and Acts 1:8), would comfort (John 14:16) and would teach and bring all things to remembrance (John 14:26).

If they had any faith in his words whatsoever, these four chapters were enough to open new heights, new dimensions and new hope for whatever was out there in the future. This was before his betrayal, before his trial, before his death and resurrection. What a loving way to prepare them for the events ahead.

"Verily, verily, I say unto you, He that believeth on me, the works that I do shall he do also: and greater, works than these shall he do; because I go unto my Father." (John 14:12) What a parallel this promise was to that of Elisha and Elijah in the Old Testament. It wasn't that Elisha was desiring to get rid of Elijah, but he knew that once Elijah was taken away that he would possess the power of Elijah in a double measure. He couldn't wait to take the prophet's mantle to the river Jordan and watch it miraculously part when he smote it (see 2 Kings 2:14). Now, the day would come when the dependent disciples would do the same works that Jesus performed because of the promised Comforter which Jesus said would be sent unto them.

Jesus said, "...the works that I do shall he do also; and *greater* works than these shall he do also." (John 14:12) Jesus said that if a man believed on him that he could do his works and be able to do even greater works once He had ascended to the Father and sent unto them the Comforter which is the Holy Ghost.

The promise of the infilling of the Holy Spirit (or Baptism with the Holy Ghost) is mentioned in Matthew 3:11; John 1:33; 7:37-39; 14:12,16-17,26; 15:26; 16:7-15; Gal 3:13-14. Even these scriptures were carry-overs from the Old Testament prophet, Joel, who declared that "...it shall come to pass afterward, that I will pour out my spirit upon all flesh; and your sons and your daughters shall prophesy, your old men shall dream dreams, your young men shall see visions: And also upon the servants and upon the handmaids in those days will I pour out my spirit." (Joel 2:28, 29)

How are we to discern when this prophecy was to be fulfilled? Actually, we would have been completely in the dark and could probably spend generation after generation arguing about the real meaning of the prophecy had not the scriptures themselves given us the time and place and the duration of such a period. It never happened in Joel's day and neither was it fulfilled in Christ's day, but fifty days after the Passover (the same week Christ was crucified, the Jews celebrated their Feast of Firstfruits).

WHY PENTECOST WAS THE CHOSEN DAY

The Feast of Firstfruits was first executed in the Old Testament (Lev. 23:9-14). It was a result of a commandment of God to show that they were putting him first in their lives. Let's take note of the entire command.

"And the Lord spake unto Moses, saying, Speak unto the children of Israel, and say unto them, When ye be come into the land which I give unto you, and shall reap the harvest thereof, then ye shall bring a sheaf [Hebrew, meaning a heap, an omer] of the firstfruits of your harvest unto the priest: and he shall wave the sheaf before the Lord, to be accepted for you: on the morrow after the Sabbath the priest shall wave it. And ye shall offer that day when ye wave the sheaf and he lamb without blemish of the first year for a burnt offering unto the Lord."

Now this was the Feast of Firstfruits which came about fifty days before the Feast of Pentecost. This feast is called "The Day of Pentecost" (Acts 2:1; 20:16). "The Feast of Harvest" (Ex. 23:16); and "The Feast of Weeks" (Ex. 34:22).

Now we can see the difference in the two celebrations. The Feast of the Firstfruits honored God, giving him first what was rightfully his. The Feast of Pentecost was a day of celebration for the people, for their share of the harvest, for their time of reaping. You'll see in just a moment what an exciting parallel these two feasts are to the crucifixion of Christ and the

Day of Pentecost of Acts 2.

A LAMB WITHOUT BLEMISH

After a sheaf of the firstfruits was waved by the priest during the Feast of Firstfruits, a perfect lamb, without blemish, was offered unto the Lord. It must be observed here that this feast was an annual event and was celebrated at the same time as the Passover (Ex. 12; 23:14-17).

Little did the world of Christ's day realize that there was a special Lamb, "without spot or blemish," whom God had withheld from the beginning to be offered upon an altar in their time, that would not only forgive their sins, but eliminate them once and for all

Jesus Christ of Nazareth was the lamb who echoed from the prophecies of Isaiah, "He was oppressed and he was afflicted, yet he opened not his mouth: he is brought as a lamb to the slaughter, and as a sheep before her shearers is dumb, so he openeth not his mouth, He was taken from prison and from judgment: and who shall declare his generation? For he was cut off out of the land of the living: for the transgression of my people was he stricken." (Isa. 53:7-8)

Jesus Christ is called "The Lamb of God" (John 1:29, 36). He is called "The lamb slain from the foundation of the world" (Rev. 13:8), indicating that the crucifixion, or the offering up of Christ on the cross was planned from the beginning. And again here now the apostle Peter refers to Him, "Forasmuch as ye know ye were not redeemed with corruptible things, as silver and gold, from your vain conversation received by tradition from your fathers; But with the precious, blood of Christ, as *a lamb without blemish and without spot*: Who verily was foreordained before the foundation of the world, but was manifest in these last times for you." (1 Peter 1:18-20, *emphasis mine*)

When the Passover and the Feast of Firstfruits was drawing near, there was a man called Jesus who lay prostrate upon the sandy face of Gethsemane. "For this cause came I into the world and unto this end was I horned" would soon come dissipating from his lips. He had but one ultimate goal in coming to this sin-cursed world, and that was to restore fallen man back into relationship with his maker by sacrificing himself on the cross of Calvary. Little did the horrid crowd of accusers and murderers realize that they were sharing in the Feast of Firstfruits by offering up the Lamb of lambs. Not one cry of despair fell from his parched lips. The scriptures declare that "He openeth not his mouth." (Isa. 53:7)

How do we know that Jesus Christ was the lamb to be offered on the Feast of Firstfruits? Because the Bible itself says that "...now is Christ risen from the dead, and *become the firstfruits* of them that slept." (1 Cor. 15:20, *emphasis mine*)

FIFTY DAYS LATER

First Corinthians 15 gives varied accounts of proof

of Christ's resurrection: "For I delivered unto you first of all that which I also received, how that Christ died for our sins according to the scriptures; And that He was buried, and that He rose again the third day according to the scriptures: And that He was seen of Cephas, then of the twelve: After that, He was seen of above five hundred brethren at once; of whom the greater part remain unto this present, but some are fallen asleep. After that, He was seen of James: then of all the apostles. And last of all He was seen of me also, as of one born out of due time." (1 Cor. 15:3-8)

After Christ arose from the grave, He walked with his disciples for forty more days before his ascension (Acts 1:3). What a man this was that even the grave loosed its power on him. Now, more than ever, those admiring, dedicated followers idolized his image, his greatness and his glory. Desiring now, more than ever to be like him, to possess his qualities and to imitate his life. How could they do it? How could it ever be possible that they, mere earthlings, could ever possess his power to do the work that He did among them? Isn't this what He had promised them in John 14? Had He not promised to them a Comforter that would abide with them forever? Indeed, He had and He was not about to forget about that promise now. Just as the prophet Elijah had fulfilled his promise to Elisha to give him a double portion of his spirit, even so now Christ reconfirms his promise to those faithful believers who stood about him.

But only forty-three days had gone by since He was offered upon the altar of all times. Forty-three days had expired since the Feast of Firstfruits. Three of those days He had spent in the heart of the earth and the other forty was spent in walking and talking with his followers (see Acts 1:3). There was yet seven days before Pentecost, "The Feast of Harvest," and what a harvest they would see. Thus Christ tells his hungry disciples that shortly the power of God would fill their lives and the prophecies of John the Baptist would be fulfilled.

"And, being assembled together with them, [Christ] commanded them that they should not depart from Jerusalem, but wait for the promise of the Father, which, saith He, ye have heard of me [*the promises of John 14*]. For John [*called John the Baptist*] truly baptized with water; but ye shall be baptized with the Holy Ghost [*the "invisible force," ruach and pneuma*] not many days hence [*seven to be exact*]. (Acts 1:4-5)

"But ye shall receive power [*the invisible force*], after that the Holy Ghost [*one and the same*] is come upon you: and ye shall be witnesses unto me both in Jerusalem, and in all Judaea, and in Samaria, and unto the uttermost part of the earth. And when He had spoke these things, while they beheld, He was taken up; and a cloud received him out' of their sight. And while they looked steadfastly toward heaven as He went up, behold, two men stood by them in white apparel; which also said, 'Ye men of Galilee, why stand ye gazing up into heaven? This same Jesus, which is taken up from you into heaven, shall so come in life manner as ye have seen him go into heaven.'" (Acts 1:8-10) From this moment, it was a matter of prayer, dedication and waiting for the ultimate fulfillment of Christ's promise. What would it be like to be like Jesus, to have his nature, his poise, his power and his strength? It was a dream worth waiting for no matter what the cost.

So, while the rest of the Jewish world prepared for the Feast of Pentecost, one hundred and twenty Spirit-hungry men and women waited in prayerful anticipation for the great moment to come. Outside the prayer room, the hustle and bustle of busy streets revealed the nearing event – a time of celebrating their harvest. But history was about to produce a harvest that it had not prepared for. The days dwindled from the calendar. Only four days to go, then three, two, one and then…

THE IMAGE OF CHRIST IS REVIVED IN THE FORM OF HIS FOLLOWERS

"And when the day of Pentecost was fully come, they were all with one accord in one place. And suddenly there came a sound from heaven as of a rushing mighty wind, and it filled all the house where they were sitting. And there appeared unto them cloven tongues like as of fire, and it sat upon each of them. And they were all filled with the Holy Ghost, and began to speak with other tongues, as the Spirit gave them utterance." (Acts 2:1-4)

The world is about to turn around on its historical axis. A transformation had taken place that man had never before witnessed. A man called Jesus Christ, full of power and wisdom, had been murdered, had rose from his grave, had ascended back to his heavenly throne and had now placed his image, his power, his strength and his personally into the lives of approximately one hundred and twenty human beings to carry on his work. What headlines it must have made in the Jerusalem Time. Something had just happened in that prayer room that could not be discounted by even the most skeptic inquirer.

"And suddenly there came a sound from heaven as of a rushing mighty wind." That alone was enough to arouse the attention, the interest of the thousands of people who had flooded the city for the festive occasion. It was difficult to explain. It sounded like a mighty wind. It filled the house where the one hundred and twenty were waiting. It then became visible in the form of dispersed, individual tongues of fire and set upon each of them. Immediately the Bible says, "And they were all filled with the Holy Ghost."

This was only the beginning of the miraculous. They now had the attention of Jerusalem. One hundred and twenty common Galileans, who a few days before would not have been able to have gained the attention of anyone, now take the center stage. All eyes are upon them and the Spirit of God makes his move. "...and began to speak with other tongues, as the Spirit gave them utterance."

TONGUES

Since "tongues" and the "unknown tongue" are two different manifestations of the Spirit, let's take them only as they come and place them in their rightful place in order to eliminate the massive confusion that exists among full Gospel believers.

We have no choice but to believe and to accept that the "tongues" in this passage (Acts 2) refer to different languages and not to the "unknown tongue." This was the first miracle that the Holy Ghost performed to convince the startled multitude that these people had received something worth taking notice of.

"And there were dwelling at Jerusalem Jews, devout men, out of every nation under heaven. Now when this was noised abroad, the multitude came together, and were confounded, [*Why?*] saying one to another, 'Behold, are not all these which speak Galileans? And how hear we every man in our own tongue [*or language as in verse 6*], wherein we were born? Parthians, and Medes, and Elamites, and the dwellers in Mesopotamia, and in Judaea, and Cappadocia, in Pontus, and Asia, Phrygia, and Pamphylia, in Egypt, and in the parts of Libya about Cyrene, and strangers of Rome, Jews and Proselytes, Cretes and Arabians, we do hear them speak in our tongues the wonderful works of God.'" (Acts 2:5-11)

It was enough to disturb any metropolitan city.

Notice all the different people who were present to witness the phenomena. The most startling mystery of all was the fact that they all understood these lowly, common Galileans speaking because they were speaking fluently in their native languages.

One of the questions at this point that I have always wondered about is what was said. "…we do hear them speak in our tongues the wonderful works of God." (vs. 11) Whatever was said, it was wonderful as the scripture states.

This would not have appeared to be a mystery had this happened on the premises of the High Priest or among scholarly men. They would have normally accepted the fact that men of this caliber had knowledge of their languages. There would have been no excitement about it whatsoever. But these were unscholarly men and women. Here were fishermen, some who were even illiterate, such as the apostle Peter who was shortly to address and astonish the crowd. Sheep herders, carpenters, housewives, fishermen were suddenly transformed mysteriously into missionaries of the gospel with an immediate use of the perspective language.

We make no reference here that they were given a supernatural knowledge of these languages. It is highly doubtful that they even knew what they were saying because they spoke, "…as the Spirit gave them utterance." (vs.4) It was the beginning of a new era in religion and it took a miracle beyond comprehension to turn the world around. People's attention had to be captured. They would have to be convinced that the man whom they crucified fifty days before was not just a carpenter's son from Nazareth, but the Son of God. To turn these people to Jesus Christ would require a direct message from God, one that could not be questioned, one that would put all the puzzle pieces together. Peter could have gone out into the streets and told them the same thing on the street corner that he preached to them in this chapter, but no one would have listened to him. But they are going to listen to him now. They've been shaken to the core of their beings. They don't understand what is happening and they're asking for answers, asking these lowly men. Listen to them:

"And they were all amazed and were in doubt, saying one to another, 'What meaneth this?' Others mocking said, 'These men are full of new wine.'" (vs. 12-13)

Now that he has their undivided attention, the onetime riverboat captain graces the speaker's spotlight: "But Peter, standing up with the eleven, lifted up his voice, and said unto them, 'Ye men of Judaea, and all ye that dwell at Jerusalem, be this known unto you, and hearken to my words: For these are not drunken, as ye suppose, seeing it is but the third hour of the day. But this is that which was spoken by the prophet Joel. And it shall come to pass in the last days, saith God, I will pour out of my Spirit upon all flesh: and your sons and your daughters shall prophesy, and your young men shall see visions, and your old men shall dream dreams: and on my servants and on my handmaidens I will pour out in those days of my Spirit; and they shall prophesy.'" (Acts 2:14-18)

Peter also continues to give the remaining parts of Joel's prophecy which is yet to be fulfilled even until this day. Of course it would be easy to fabricate interpretations for the "...wonders in heaven above, and signs in the earth beneath; blood and fire, and vapour of smoke. The sun shall be turned into darkness, and the moon into blood before that great notable day of the Lord come." (vs. 19-20) But these prophecies are yet to be fulfilled and will not be fulfilled until the tribulation period (Rev. 6:12; 8:12; 9:2; 16:10; Matt. 24:29). As a matter of fact he says that these things would happen just "...before that great and notable day of the Lord come." This doesn't refer to the rapture of the Saints but to the time when Christ returns to earth at the end of the seven year tribulation period to set up his thousand year kingdom upon the earth. This is referred to as the Great Day of the Lord (Rev. 1:7; 2 Peter 3:10; 2 Thess. 2:2).

PETER CONVINCES THEM OF CHRIST

"Ye men of Israel, hear these words: Jesus of Nazareth, a man approved of God among you by miracles and wonders and signs, which God did by him in the midst of you, as ye yourselves also know: him being delivered by the determinate counsel and foreknowledge of God, ye have taken, and by wicked hands have crucified and slain: Whom God hath raised up, having loosed the pains of death: because it was not possible that He should be holden of it." (vs. 22-24)

"This Jesus hath God raised up, whereof we all are witnesses. Therefore being by the right hand of God exalted, and having received of the Father the promise of the Holy Ghost, He hath shed forth this, which ye now see and hear." (vs. 32-33)

Everything they were now witnessing was a direct answer to prophecy and the promises of Jesus Christ which He made in John 14. He said that Jesus had "...received of the Father the promise of the Holy Ghost [*the comforter, the invisible force*], He hath shed forth this which ye now see and hear."

"Therefore let all the house of Israel know assuredly, that God hath made that same Jesus, whom ye have crucified, both Lord and Christ." (vs. 36)

This was the clincher. Suddenly they realize the familiarity in the voices and actions of these one hundred and twenty men and women. They had the same air, the same forcefulness as the man Jesus whom Peter was speaking of. Fifty days before they had crucified a man called Jesus, believing him to be an imposter, a trouble maker and a law breaker. Now, they have been made to realize that the man whom they had killed was indeed the Son of God. Their eyes are immediately opened to the awesome truth and they were pricked to their hearts.

"Now when they heard this, they were pricked in their heart, and said unto Peter and to the rest of the apostles, 'Men and brethren, what shall we do?'" (vs. 37)

What did they mean, "What shall we do?" They had committed the crime of crimes and had just been made to realize it. They were sorry. The scriptures say, "...they were pricked in their heart." They wanted to know what they could do to undo what they had done. This point must be understood to interpret the following verse because everything hinges upon it. In fact, they wanted to ask forgiveness of their hideous crime but didn't know where to begin. Peter, then, tells them in a few detailed words the solution to their inquiry.

"Then Peter said unto them, Repent..." Not because they did not believe in God, for they were already considered devoted followers of God. (vs. 2:5) They were there in Jerusalem following a tradition which God himself had commanded them. Many had come from hundreds of miles with great sacrifice to honor their Lord's command. The crime that they were guilty of was done in ignorance. They were to repent of what they had done because God isn't set on judgment because He "...is longsuffering to us-ward, not willing that any should perish, but that all should come to repentance." (2 Peter 3:9)

Jehovah God they knew and believed upon, but

Peter tells them to repent and accept Jesus Christ as Savior. This is what is meant by "Repent and be baptized every one of you in the name of Jesus Christ for the remission of sins..." (vs. 38) This "baptism" was not a baptism in water. Nothing is said of water in these verses. This "baptism" was one which could take away sins. He states that it was for "...the remission of sins." Water baptism has never taken away sins. John the Baptist refused to baptize anyone in water who had not already been forgiven of sins (see Matt. 3:7-8). Simon believed and was baptized in water and his heart was still not right with God (see Acts 8:13-22).

The "baptism" mentioned here in Acts 2:38 would take away sins and there is not but one baptism (Eph. 4:5) which can do that and it is a spiritual baptism, a baptism into Christ (Rom 6:33-34; Gal 3:27).

ACCESS TO ALL THE FULLNESS OF GOD

The Feast of Harvest was on this day. It was called the Day of Pentecost (meaning 50) because it was fifty days after the Passover and the Feast of Firstfruits when the Lamb without blemish was offered up. Yes, this was the Day of Harvest and what a harvest they did reap. Three thousand people turned to Christ and accepted him as Lord and Savior (vs. 41) while the fear of God fell upon the rest of them.

While this city-wide revival entranced Jerusalem and souls were confessing and accepting Christ, the power of Jesus Christ through the infilling of the Holy

Ghost caused miracles and wonders to be performed through the apostles. The thing which they had always desired had come to pass. They wanted to be like Jesus, have his courage, his power and his ability. All of it had come through the promise of the Holy Ghost. They were so endowed with the image of Christ until they were later called "Christians" (Acts 11:26) which comes from the Greek word "Christianos" meaning "followers of Christ."

WERE THERE LIMITATIONS?

Was this outpouring of the Spirit only a one day affair? Were the disciples only privileged to possess the image and power of Christ for a day? For a promise that had been so long prophesied and so profoundly promised, it doesn't seem right that God would give them such a taste of the supernatural for only a day or a week. To whom was the promise made and to how many and for what period of time? Peter answered this question during his message to the inquiring crowd in verse 39: "For the promise is unto you, and to your children, and to all that are afar off, even as many as the Lord our God shall call."

Joel's prophecy of this event was given almost 800 years prior to Acts 2. Over 4,000 years had expired since the creation of Adam. It is only interesting to note these figures of years to establish a point. The "last days," as we have so often read the term in the scriptures, would have to refer to the last era or dispensation of time. The flood of Noah's day concluded the first 2,000 year period from Adam. The flood until the birth of Christ was another 2,000 years making a total of 4,000 years. Thus, the second 2,000 year period (from the flood until Christ) could not have been the "last days." The fact that the end of time didn't come is proof within itself. But today we find ourselves in the latter part of the third 2,000 year period which began either with Christ or Acts 2. We have no proof to say which of the two events that the latter 2,000 year period began with, but we do know that Joel's prophecy 800 years before stated that the events in Acts 2 were to occur in "the last days." Whether with Christ or the Day of Pentecost doesn't really matter that much since there is only about 33 years difference in the two events. What is important is that we are now living in "the last days." We don't have ample time at this point of our book to give a complete explanation or proof, but it appears to be a definite, prophetic prognostication that the year 2000 A.D. would find us very close to the end of this age. Of course we are still waiting and anticipating the coming of Jesus Christ. If this suggests to you that we don't have much time left, then you understand clearly why we are interested in getting this gospel preached throughout the world now.

TO ALL THAT ARE AFAR OFF

The events recorded in Acts 2:42-47 suggest that at

least several days, or weeks, expired before the events of the following chapter. But just as the prophet Elisha was anxious to use his newly acquired powers, so the disciples also were unrestrained in testing their image of the man from Galilee. The events beginning in chapter three tells it all. Going up to the temple at the hour of prayer, Peter and John were halted by a lame man at the gate of the temple. There is a question to be asked at this point to the people of our day. What good is there in having the power of Christ to rest upon us if we cannot meet the needs of people? Why should the poor and hungry be left to someone else to provide for them? Why should the sick and suffering only receive our pity and get well cards? Why have Jesus Christ in our lives and yet tie his hands from meeting the needs of the people which He so desires? Christ works through us with the power of the Holy Ghost. And herein lays the purpose of being filled with the Holy Spirit – to do the works of Jesus Christ.

"And a certain man lame from his mother's womb was carried, whom they laid daily at the gate of the temple which is called Beautiful, to ask alms of them that entered into the temple: Who seeing Peter and John about to go into the temple asked an alms. And Peter, fastening his eyes upon him with John, said, "look on us.'" (Acts 3:2-4)

This has been a most fascinating statement to me, "Look on us." It takes real courage, faith and knowing where you stand with God, to tell the world to look at you as though you have the answers and solutions to their problems. Don't ever tell people to look to you for help unless you're able to produce it.

But these men could produce. They now possessed the Spirit, power and the image of Jesus Christ. They were ready to fulfill Christ's promise in John 14, "...the work that I do, ye shall do also and greater..." How? Through the indwelling of the Holy Ghost and being confident of what they possessed

"Then Peter said, 'Silver and gold have I none; but such as I have give I thee: In the name of Jesus Christ of Nazareth rise up and walk.'"

"And he took him by the right hand, lifted him up: and immediately his feet and ankle bones received strength. And he leaping up stood, and walked, and entered with them into the temple, walking and leaping, and praising God." (Acts 3:6-8)

This miracle once again brought the people together in amazement giving way for another sermon from Peter which resulted in another harvest of 5,000 souls (vs. 4:4). The power of Christ working through them had already converted more people with two sermons than they had seen in the three years of Christ's earthly ministry.

After several confrontations with the authorities of the city and being threatened because of their exploits and use of the name of "Jesus," they continued their ministry with more converted and filled with the Holy Ghost (vs. 4:31). To this point we know that the outpouring of the Spirit was not just for those on Pentecost Day. Peter had said, "…for the promise is to you and to your children…"

Quite a period of time now elapses between this chapter and chapter eight. Most of this time records persecution against God's people. The old die-hards, who thought they had rid themselves of the meddling Galilean by nailing him to the cross, now find that He is more alive than ever through the miraculous exploits of his disciples. They are preaching the same doctrine, performing the same miracles and disturbing the same people. Christ was now magnified and multiplied through the power of the Holy Ghost.

An undetermined period of time goes by until we come to Acts 8. Philip, one of the deacons of his day, went to the city of Samaria to preach to them Jesus. "And the people with one accord gave heed unto those things which Philip spake, hearing and seeing the miracles which he did. For unclean spirits, crying with loud voices came out of many that were possessed with them: and many taken with palsies, and that were lame, were healed. And there was great joy in that city." (Acts 8:6-8)

But this was only the beginning. People were being converted, healed and delivered of demon oppression and possession, but there was more to come for them. First Corinthians 12:13 says, "For by one Spirit are we all baptized into one body," but this is only referring to our spiritual baptism or our conversion. At that point we become a child of God and the Spirit places us into the spiritual body of Christ as a part of him.

Verse 12 says both men and women *believed* and were *baptized*. It is very safe to assume that these were saved and born again people. But as we have said, God had more for them. Once they had become children of God, they had access to the same power, the same "invisible force," the same image of Christ, as Philip and the apostles.

"Now when the apostles which were at Jerusalem heard that Samaria had received the word of God, they sent unto them Peter and John: Who, when they were come down, prayed for them, that they might receive the Holy Ghost: For as yet he was fallen upon none of them: only they were baptized in the name of the Lord Jesus." (Acts 8:14-16)

This is probably months after Pentecost. Yet, the Spirit is still being poured out. And this scripture alone (there are others) proves that the infilling, or baptism of the Holy Ghost, is separate and apart from conversion. Peter and John had gone down to Samaria to pray for the new converts that they also may be filled with the Holy Ghost because "For as yet He (the Holy Ghost) was fallen upon none of them: only they were baptized in the name of the Lord Jesus."

Let's continue here and see the results of their prayers. "Then laid they their hands on them, and they received the Holy Ghost." (vs. 17)

We don't mean to imply that one cannot receive

the Holy Ghost at the time of conversion because the apostle Paul is an example of one who did (Acts 9:17-18). But it is clear from the scriptures that it is a separate experience from conversion.

On the Day of Pentecost, the one hundred and twenty received the Holy Ghost and 3,000 were saved. A few days later 5,000 were saved and more received the Holy Ghost. Several months later (chapter 8) men and women received the Holy Ghost in Samaria after being saved and baptized.

Now eight years goes by from the second chapter of Acts until the tenth chapter where we now pick up. Peter is instructed by the Lord to go to Caesarea to preach to a family of Gentiles, to the household of Cornelius.

The scriptures say that Cornelius was "...a centurion of the band called the Italian band, a devout man, and one that feared God with all his house, which gave much alms to the people, and prayed to God always." (Acts 10:1-2)

A man can be devoted to his country, as was Cornelius; he may give freely to charity, as did Cornelius; he may pray a great deal and fear God, but this still does not constitute a born-again experience. A man cannot be saved until he comes to the knowledge of the truth (1 Timothy 2:4). Those who were converted on the day of Pentecost were already religious people and devoted to Jehovah (Acts 2:5) but they didn't come to the knowledge of Jesus Christ and his saving power until Peter enlightened them with his sermon.

"And as Peter was coming in, Cornelius met him, and fell down at his feet, and worshipped him. But Peter took him up, saying, Stand up; I myself also am a man. And as he talked with him, he went in, and found many that were come together. And he said unto them, 'Ye know how that it is an unlawful thing for a man that is a Jew to keep company, or come unto one of another nation; but God hath shewed me that I should not call any man common or unclean. Therefore came I unto you without gainsaying, as soon as I was sent for: I ask therefore for what intent ye have sent for me?'" (Acts 10:25-29)

Cornelius then explains to Peter how the Lord instructed him during a time of fasting and prayer, to send men to Joppa to inquire of him that he may come and speak to them whatsoever God commanded him. "Now therefore are we all here present before God to hear all things that are commanded thee of God." (vs. 33)

Peter then turned and addressed the crowded house. He gave them the simple plan of salvation beginning with the person of Jesus Christ, his life, death and what He could do through his resurrection.

"While Peter yet spake these words, the Holy Ghost fell on all them which heard the word." (vs. 44) Here is another example of men and women receiving the Holy Ghost at the time of their conversion. But conversion itself comes by believing on the Lord Jesus Christ as Peter had just stated in verse 43. Was this outpouring of the Spirit the same as that which was poured out eight years earlier at Pentecost?

"And they of the circumcision which believed were astonished, as many as came with Peter, because that on the Gentiles also was poured out the gift of the Holy Ghost." (vs.45) The word "also" indicates the comparison between what the Jews had received and what now the Gentiles had received. Was there any kind of unusual manifestation that accompanied the outpouring of the Spirit as was the case at Pentecost? There were no numerous gathering of languages here to hear in different "tongues." Yet, there was a similarity here that convinced the men who came with Peter that this outpouring was the same as at Pentecost. What was that similarity?

"For they heard them speak with tongues, and magnify God. Then answered Peter, 'Can any man forbid water, that these should not be baptized, which have received the Holy Ghost as well as we?' And he commanded them to be baptized in the name of the Lord. Then prayed they him to tarry certain days." (vs. 46-48)

This proves that the Holy Ghost endowment can be given at the time of conversion as was also in the case of Paul (Acts 9:17-18) or long after the time of conversion as in the case of the disciples at Pentecost (Acts 2:1-11), the Samaritans (Acts 8:12-23), and the Ephesians (Acts 19:1-7). We also have proof here that one can receive the Holy Ghost before water baptism as was also in Paul's case (Acts 9:17-18), or after baptism as it was with Jesus (Matt. 3:16-17), the disciples at Pentecost (Acts 2), the Samaritans (Acts 8:4-23) and the Ephesians (Acts 19:1-7).

In any case, the 800 year old prophecy of Joel (Joel 2:28) and the prophecy of Christ (John 14:12-17,26; Acts 1:8) had now been poured out on both Jews and Gentiles alike over a period of eight years. But the outpouring did not stop. There are no scriptures to substantiate the claims that the Spirit outpouring was a one-time event. The infilling of the Holy Ghost continued and is evidenced fifteen years later (from Acts 10), twenty-three years from the Day of Pentecost in the account of Acts 19.

"And it came to pass, that, while Apollos was at Corinth, Paul having passed through the upper coast came to Ephesus: and finding certain disciples. He said unto them, 'Have ye received the Holy Ghost since ye believed? And they said unto him, 'We have not so much as heard whether there be any Holy Ghost.'" (Acts 19:1-2)

Here Paul verifies that the Baptism of the Holy Ghost to be a separate experience from conversion. "Have ye received the Holy Ghost since ye believed?" was his inquiry.

"And they said unto him, 'We have not so much as heard whether there be any Holy Ghost.' And he said unto them, 'Unto what then were ye baptized?' And they said, 'Unto John's baptism.'" (vs. 2-3)

It isn't really clear here who these men were. They are called disciples and there were twelve of them (vs. 1 and 12). It appears that they were not acquainted with

Jesus but they knew of John the Baptist. Since Ephesus is almost a thousand miles from where John preached, he couldn't have preached to them in person if they were Ephesians. They could have been followers of John's doctrine as was the learned Apollos in the previous chapter (Acts 18:24-25) or they could well have been missionaries of John the Baptist and had been absent from Jerusalem since his death. This would explain their discipleship and their knowledge of John, the lack of knowledge of Jesus or Pentecost and their purpose of being in Ephesus. But John the Baptist had told his followers, "I indeed baptize you with water unto repentance, but He who cometh after me, who is mightier than I shall baptize you with the Holy Ghost and with fire." Why didn't they remember those words? Certainly, if they were John's disciples, they should have known. But then again, twenty-six years is a long time and things are easily forgotten. However, the Lord does not forget and He had not forgotten these men. He has his own way of routing his messengers in the direction of those who are in need.

"Then said Paul, 'John verily baptized with the baptism of repentance, saying unto the people, that they should believe on him which should come after him, that is, on Christ Jesus.' When they heard this, they were baptized in the name of the Lord Jesus. And when Paul had laid his hands upon them, the Holy Ghost came on them; and they spake with tongues, and prophesied." (vs. 4-6)

Two manifestations of the Spirit accompanied the

Spirit baptism here and we will get into that in just a little while. But at this point, we're only trying to point out that "...when the day of Pentecost had fully come..." there are no scriptural evidences that it ever "fully went." There was no limit of time, generation or era. Peter had not only stated "...for the promise is to you and to your children but also "to all who are afar off [*generations to come*] even as many as the Lord our God shall call [*or save*]." (Acts 2:39)

THE HOLY GHOST TODAY

The Holy Ghost is still being poured out into the hearts of believers today to accomplish the same purposes as it did in those days. The Spirit has never gone into seclusion during any "dark ages" as some have taught. Men and women who went through the perils of persecution in Rome were tortured, murdered and given to wild, hungry beasts, died, but died in the faith with the Holy Ghost speaking through them during their last fleeting breaths.

During the Reformation days in Germany, the Holy Ghost worked through the lives of thousands of Christians who were martyred for the cause of Christ. However, no matter what comes or goes, God will have a remnant of people who will hold on until the end. These blessed warriors of the faith are those who hold the banner of truth until victory overtakes in a revival of success. Certainly, God's people have come through fire and deep waters. It is true that many have fallen by the wayside. It is also true that many have been tempted astray into a change of beliefs, but somewhere in the crowd there's one, or a few, who still hold the treasure of God close to their breast and will soon be credited in bringing a revival once again.

Some are careless and egotistical enough to believe that their church or organization brought a revival of the "Spirit Outpouring" in the early 1900s, but for them to believe such, they would have to completely discount what Christ said when He said, "...and he shall give you another Comforter, that he may abide with you *forever*." When the Spirit came, He came to stay. He never left once He came. He never went underground and delved himself into any dark ages. He has been the comforter to the comfortless, the power to the powerless, and the image of Christ to the converted. He is the power of God in men to do the works of Jesus.

"...God anointed Jesus of Nazareth with the Holy Ghost and with power: who went about doing good, and healing all that were oppressed of the devil; for God was with him" (Acts 10:38)

"For even hereunto were ye called: because Christ also suffered for us, leaving us an example, that ye should follow his steps." (1 Peter 2:21)

The Holy Ghost is still being poured out to those believers today in order to accomplish the same purposes as it did in those early days. They desired to do what Christ did. They wanted the same supernatural security as Christ: his strength, his wisdom, his ability to do the works of God, his character and poise, and his intimacy with the Divine. It wasn't beyond reality because it was promised to them. Not only was it promised to them but also to us today who have been chosen of the Lord and cleansed by his blood and made heirs of his grace.

DON'T BE FOOLED

Let us concede right now that "Pentecostalism," as it has been called, has suffered unduly because of the wrong image that has been splattered across it's holy path by careless, unwise, ignorant and thoughtless perverts who have used its cloak for their "medicine show revivals," their "snake handling sideshows" and money making schemes. Satan is a shrewd operator. He never uses the unreal for his platform. His delight is taking the faultless, the spotless and the holy to transform his agents into "angels of light" and eventually use them to discount the virtues of God's dedicated disciples.

Romans 5:5 says: "...the love of God is shed abroad in our hearts by the Holy Ghost which is given unto us." And that love "...suffereth long, and is kind; envieth not: vaunteth not itself, is not puffed up. Doth not behave itself unseemly, seeketh not her own, is not easily provoked, thinketh no evil; Rejoiceth not in iniquity, but rejoiceth in the truth; Beareth all things, believeth all things, hopeth all things, endureth all things." (1 Corinthians 13:4-7)

Here is the ingredient for separating the good from the bad, the fake from the real, and the godly from the ungodly. *You* become the deciding factor. Will the real Christian please stand up? Or are there those who could care less about projecting the image of Christ? Where is the man who has no desire for the supernatural working of God in his life? Where is the woman who believes that she can make it through life under her own strength? Who dares to disbelieve that Jesus Christ is the same, yesterday, and forever? Who can be satisfied to read of the divine exploits in the New Testament and not believe to see the same manifestations of the Spirit in these days?

It is a fact that men find answers when they look for them. Jesus made this philosophy a part of his preaching when He walked the face of this earth long ago (see Matt. 7:7). Closing one's eyes to that which is truth doesn't eliminate the truth; it merely places a barrier between you and the truth. Closing one's eyes doesn't suffice for a cloak of ignorance. The scriptures are plain, God's promises are clear and you are the only final deciding factor.

But doesn't it seem appropriate to accept the fact that if we can be forgiven of our sins, made to become the sons and daughters of God through the new birth, placed into the Body of Jesus Christ and called Christians after his name, that we should not desire to do his work and be partakers of his divine nature?

A FULLNESS OF THE SPIRIT

It has already been made clear that one does not

receive the fullness of the Spirit or a baptism in the Spirit at the time of his conversion, as some men teach. To believe this, one would have to concede that none of the one hundred and twenty disciples at Pentecost were converted until they received the Spirit. Then, of course, there are those who even believe this line of thinking. But to believe that, one would have to believe that the thief on the cross was lost despite the fact that Jesus promised to see him the same day in Paradise. The twelve disciples in Acts 19 were saved twenty-six years before ever hearing about the baptism of the Holy Ghost.

When one is converted, he receives the Sprit by measure but has not yet obtained the Spirit in his fullness. Jesus confirmed this in one of his promises to the disciples in John 14:17: "Even the Spirit of Truth whom the world cannot receive, because it seeth him not, neither knoweth him; but ye know him; for he dwelleth with you [*at that time*], and shall [*future, at Pentecost*] be in you."

HOW TO RECEIVE THE HOLY GHOST

The scriptures are not nearly as complicated as theologians have made them to be. Pentecostals, too, have warped conceptions about being filled with the Spirit although they are very much acquainted with his work. It is only fortunate for some that God understands the limitations of man and how easy it is for him to fall into traditionalism. He desires to be filled with the Holy Ghost and has been fed all of the so-called "old-fashioned" methods and formulas for receiving his blessing from God. This awesome scene can be magnified, and expanded upon easily. He's told that he has to pray and pray and pray at the altar until the blessing comes. People gather around him, shouting in his ears, beating him on the back, breathing in his face, telling him to hold on, turn loose, raise his hands, stand to his feet, say "Praise God! Praise God!" clap his hands, etc. And the poor fellow returns to his pew exhausted, bewildered, discouraged because he did everything that was told him, and did it in good faith and in all good conscience, and yet, for some unseen reason (he is told) there is something in his life that has caused God to withhold the blessing from him.

I have my doubts about such people who say they have received the Holy Ghost when they have been worked up into an emotional ecstasy. This is not to say that emotions don't have their place. But I've seen this type of expression exhibited among the heathen, dancing to the sound of drums until they would fall out in a trance and yet there was nothing godly or spiritual involved.

No place in the scriptures do we find this type of combination for unlocking the windows of heaven to receive the infilling of the Spirit. The one-hundred and twenty were the only people that were commanded to tarry for the Holy Ghost because until then He had not yet been given. But from the time the Holy Ghost was poured out at Pentecost until this present day, He has made himself available to every born-again child of God who desires his presence in their lives. He is not received by works of righteousness or by physical dexterity or emotional chants, but through faith in the promises of God.

ONLY ONE FORMULA GIVEN

The simplest method ever given was given by Christ himself: "If ye then, being evil [*earthly*], know how to give good gifts unto your children: how much more shall your heavenly Father give the Holy Spirit to them that ask him?" (Luke 11:13)

Acts 2:38 confirms that the promises of John 14 and Luke 11:18 was a gift of God. A gift is not a gift if one must work for it. What price is there to pay? Your sins are under the blood of Jesus because He has already paid the price. The only thing He asks you to do is to believe and to receive the Holy Ghost. Why is that so complicated for people today to understand? Ask him to fill you with his Spirit and He will gladly meet the desire of your heart right now.

Receiving the Holy Ghost into your life is just as simple as receiving your salvation. You received your salvation through faith in the promises of God. You read the scriptures that said "repent" and you repented. You read 1 John 1:9: "If we confess our sins, he is faithful and just to forgive us our sins, and to cleanse us from all unrighteousness." You believed in what it said and as a result your sins were forgiven and you received Christ into your heart. But how did you know that you were converted? How could you be certain that you were saved and that your sins were truly under the blood of Jesus? Did you wait a week or so before confessing before men that you received Christ? Did you wait to see if you were delivered from all of your habits before testifying of your conversion? No, a thousand times no! You accepted Christ the very moment you came to him. You knew that you were saved because you believed in his Word. He had promised to forgive if you would confess. You confessed, and God forgave. You didn't know this as a result of lightning and thunder from heaven or handwriting on the wall. You knew it because the Word had said it and you believed it in that very moment.

There is no difference whatsoever in receiving the infilling of the Spirit and receiving your salvation. Read the scriptures. Both are received by asking and believing. That's it.

THE MANIFESTATIONS OF THE SPIRIT

Now we come to the critical part. We have traditional hurdles that we must now cross. What about the evidence of the Holy Ghost?

Don't think for one moment that I am not walking softly across this stepping stone. We have no intentions of denying any part of the works of the Spirit, but we do desire to put everything it its rightful place.

What do we mean by "evidence?" Isn't the word synonymous to the word "proof?" So then, we are being asked, "What is the proof of the Spirit?" First of all, to whom are we supposed to prove anything to? (Of course, you understand, I am following the traditional line at this moment.) What purpose would anyone have in proving to someone else that we had the fullness of the Spirit? So far, things are starting to get a little cloudy. Well, this is only to be expected when you get down to the real nitty-gritty of the facts. And I've always been one to believe that when something doesn't sound right, then it deserves to be questioned.

What about tongues? Aren't tongues the real evidence, or proof, that one is filled with the Spirit? Before we answer that question, let's examine 1 Corinthians 12.

"Now there are diversities of gifts, but the same Spirit [*Holy Ghost*], and there are differences of administrations, but the same Lord. And there are diversities of operations [*ways that the Spirit works*] but it is the same God which worketh all in all. But the manifestations [*which are about to be listed*] is given to every man to profit withal. For to one is given by the Spirit the word of wisdom; to another the word of knowledge by the same Spirit; to another faith by the same Spirit; to another gifts of healing by the same Spirit; to another the working of miracles; to another prophecy; to another discerning of spirits; to another divers kinds of tongues; to another the interpretation of tongues: but all these worketh that one and the selfsame Spirit [*Holy Ghost*], dividing to every man severally as he will." (1 Cor. 12:4-11]

All of these gifts just mentioned are manifestations of the Spirit. The word "manifest" comes from the Greek word, "phanerosis" which means, "expression" and from "phaneroo" meaning "show himself." Thus, when the Bible declares that these are manifestations of the Spirit (vs.7), it is telling us that these are the channels through which the Holy Ghost "expresses" and "shows himself" to man. But notice, I said, "channels." There is no one who could expressly pinpoint a definite blueprint as to the different ways these manifestations can work. You just read that: "there are diversities [*different ways*] of operations."

Now it is a fact that "tongues" were a manifestation of the Spirit. Examine, if you will, those incidents recorded in the scriptures where men spoke with tongues (see Acts 2:4,11; 10:44-48; 19:1-7). But these statements do not answer your question: "What is the evidence of the infilling of the Holy Ghost?" Or "Are tongues the evidence of the Holy Ghost?"

You can understand better if we use the term, "proof" instead of "evidence," although they mean the same thing. The word, "proof" comes from the Greek, "tekmar" meaning "a token of facts or criterion of certainty, unquestionable evidence." Thus, let's put our questions to the test and see if they can stand.

If "tongues" were proof that one was filled with the Holy Ghost, then all who speak with tongues would have the Holy Ghost within. But you say, "I don't believe that everyone who speaks with tongues has the Spirit of God in them." But they speak with tongues, do they not? If it is evidence, or proof, for one person, it would have to be proof for another. Does that sound right to you? If not, then I know what you mean.

The apostle Paul said that a man could speak with tongues and not have the love of God within him (1 Cor. 13:1). Inasmuch as Satan can imitate these manifestations of the Spirit, they then, do not prove anything to anybody. The manifestations of the Spirit were never meant to be proof of anything, only to be used by the Spirit-filled Christians to "profit" in the kingdom of God. (1 Cor. 12:7)

Spirit-filled Christians may speak with tongues, but all who speak with tongues are not necessarily filled with the Spirit. So then, our traditional idea about "evidence" doesn't hold water. So let's talk about real evidences. Take note now that real, genuine Spirit-filled people are not concerned about proving to anyone whether or not the Holy Ghost abides within. The "proofs" are for your benefit in the light of discerning others, not showing yourself to others. The proofs that we are about to give, are for your welfare in discerning whether or not the people with whom you deal are Spirit-filled, and in turn, they may be able to discern you for their own spiritual welfare.

EVIDENCES OF THE SPIRIT-FILLED LIFE

I cannot tell one tree from the other simply by the looks of the bark on them. They all have a trunk and they all have branches. In time they all have leaves which come and go. But I cannot tell the difference in trees by these characteristics. But this I do know, that when I see apples hanging from the branches on a tree, no one is going to convince me that it's a peach tree. I know better, because I can see the fruit on that tree. Those apples are the only proof and the only evidence that I need to convince me that it's an apple tree.

The way you're made doesn't prove anything. The way you look doesn't prove anything. What you say doesn't prove anything. But the way you live, the fruits of your life, do prove everything about you. Satan may imitate any of the gifts of the Spirit mentioned in 1 Cor. 12, but he can never imitate the real proofs of a Spirit-filled life that we are about to unveil to you right now.

In Galatians 5, Paul gives the "evidences" for both sides of the fence. He gives the fruits, or proofs, of the flesh and the fruits, or proofs, of the Spirit.

"Now the works of the flesh are manifest [*expressed and revealed*], which are these; adultery, fornication, uncleanness, lasciviousness, idolatry, witchcraft, hatred, variance, emulations, wrath, strife, seditions, heresies, envying, murders, drunkenness, reveling, and such like: of which I tell you before, as I have also told you in time past, that they which do such things shall not inherit the kingdom of God." (Galatians 5:19-21)

Here are seventeen "works of the flesh" listed which become proofs in one's life, that he or she is not of God. Paul said that they could never inherit the Kingdom of God as long as they produced these fruits.

However, he follows this up with the real "evidences" of a Spirit-filled person: "But the fruit [*evidence or proof*] of the Spirit is love, joy, peace, longsuffering, gentleness, goodness, faith, meekness, temperance: against such there is no law." (Galatians 5:22-23)

Now, if you think for one moment that Satan can imitate these, then you had better think again. Look at these evidences for a moment. A Spirit-filled Christian has love. Romans 5:5 says, "...the love God is shed abroad in our hearts by the Holy Ghost which is given unto us." Now anyone can lust. Anyone can love a lovable person. But no one except a Spirit-filled person can follow the commandment of Christ and love their enemies and pray for those who despitefully use them. That kind of love *only* comes through the Spirit.

If a person claims to have the Spirit in their lives just because they speak with tongues yet have hate in their hearts against someone, they stand in danger of lying to the Holy Ghost and mocking the truths of God's Word. There is no way they can have the precious Spirit of God within them and have hate at the same time.

Paul says that the Spirit-filled life has joy. Peter describes our experience with God as "Joy unspeakable and full of glory." (1 Pet. 1:8) God's people are not disgruntled. They are not the long-faced grumblers that some seem to think they're supposed to be. They are not the fault-finders or pessimists. They have joy. They look on the bright side of life and look for the best in their fellow man.

The Spirit-filled life is one of peace. Here is a man or a woman who is in control of themselves. They're not worried about circumstances, they have learned to master circumstances with faith in God's Word. The cares of the world take a backseat and they are in the driver's seat. They have nothing to fear because their sins are under the blood of Jesus. They have been baptized in his body (1 Cor. 12:13) and filled with the Holy Ghost. They have every reason to have peace in their hearts. Only a Spirit-filled life can have peace in the mist of storm.

The next proof was longsuffering. When Paul used this word, he used the Greek word, "makrothumos" which means "enduring temper." There are people who pride themselves in being hard. They somehow feel that God is proud of them for walking a straight line and keeping their neighbors in the selfsame attitude. "Kick 'em out if they don't line up," they say. "Get in or get out." Oh, they feel proud of themselves when they rid themselves of an erring member in the church as though God has used them to purge the flock. This kind of attitude is a stink in the nostrils of Almighty God.

Remember those words of 1 Corinthians 13:4: "love suffereth long?" That's the meaning of longsuffering. The same people who want God to be patient with them, don't want to pass it on to their fellowmen. How often has the Spirit reminded me of Psalms 103:10-12:

"He hath not dealt with us after our sins; nor rewarded us according to our iniquities. For as the heaven is high above the earth, so great is his mercy [*longsuffering*] toward them that fear him. As far as the east is from the west, so far hath he removed our transgressions from us."

A man who has no sympathy, no pity, no patience, no longsuffering, no forbearance to one who is weak in the faith, only opens his life to others to show his lack of evidence of a Spirit-filled life.

These fruits cannot be imitated. There are more: "gentleness, goodness, faith, meekness and temperance." These are nine infallible proofs of a Spirit-filled life.

GIFTS OF THE SPIRIT

The gifts mentioned in 1 Corinthians 12 are nine channels through which the Holy Ghost can work through you. They are all supernatural and come by the same Spirit (vs. 4). Any of these gifts can operate through a Spirit-filled person. There is no evidence that these gifts need be resident in one's life. The Holy Ghost is resident already in one's life and the gifts can operate through him whenever needed and for whatever purpose. It is true that some claim to have the gift of healing or the gift of prophecy, etc., but all that is really important is that you have the gift of the Holy Ghost. The gifts will operate whenever they're needed if you're submissive to the Spirit. So, when you ask me if a Spirit-filled person speaks with tongues, I can say, "Yes," because it is one of the manifestations of the Spirit, but I also want to point out that tongues are not necessarily evidence or proof of a Spirit-filled life.

THE OPERATIONS OF THE GIFTS

The gift of the word of wisdom is not a common attribute. This is a supernatural gift of wisdom that can only come by the Spirit. It includes having the ability to advise with God's Word in such a way as not to offend. Paul displayed this word of wisdom over and again as he pleaded his defense before his accusers. Take special notice of his shrewdness and wisdom in approaching Agrippa in Acts 26. The entire book of Hebrews was written with master wisdom which could only come from the Spirit to convince the Jew that Jesus was the Christ. It was wisdom that Paul never used his name or gave any evidence of his identity throughout the entire book. The gift of the word of wisdom is revealed in Paul's words:

"For though I be free from all men, yet have I made myself servant unto all, that I might gain the more. And unto the Jews I became as a Jew, that I might gain the Jews; to them that are under the law, as under the law, that I might gain them that are under the law." (1 Cor. 9:19-20) To the weak became I as weak, that I might gain the weak: I am made all things to all men that I might by all means save some." (vs. 22)

This is supernatural wisdom that can only come from the Spirit. The Word of God, coming from the lips of a careless and unwise mind, can be offensive and defeat its own purpose.

The gift of the word of knowledge is frequently misunderstood by readers and theologians alike. If this knowledge was simply the ability of knowing the Bible, then it would be quite evident that a person would not have to be a Christian to possess it. There are many learned men of our day who quote frequently from the Bible but have no experience with God. Lawyers often use biblical quotations in court as well as noted statesmen. Keep in mind that the gifts of the Spirit are supernatural, which indicates that they are a result of another power other than man. We often refer to the Greek in our definition of words since the New Testament was translated from that language and reference to the Greek gives us a more clear and concise revelation of the words in doubt. The word, "knowledge" is derived from two words, "ginosko" and "gnosis." The first means a "spiritual perception" and the other "the act of knowing." The gift of word of knowledge has the same connotation as having the mind of Christ that Paul mentions in Philippians 2:5.

Through the gift of the word of knowledge one may have spiritual perception just as Christ had and is recorded in so many passages of the Bible. Let's take note of a few:

"Then Jesus said unto them, Take heed and beware of the leaven of the Pharisees and of the Sadducees. And they reasoned among themselves, saying, 'It is because we have taken no bread.' Which when Jesus perceived, he said unto them, 'O ye of little faith, why reason ye among yourselves, because ye have brought no bread?'" (Matt. 16:6-8)

Jesus did not overhear them speaking. No one told him what they were talking about. He had a spiritual perception that revealed it to him. God knows all things and everything that goes on. That knowledge can be spiritually transferred to a man through the Spirit. Notice again:

In Capernaum there was a certain man who was sick with the palsy who was lowered through a rooftop in order to be healed of Jesus. The crowd was so great; it was the only way to reach him. To their surprise, Jesus forgave the man of his sins before he made him whole and this brought dissension among the hearers.

"When Jesus saw their faith, he said unto the sick of the palsy, 'Son, they sins be forgiven thee.' But there were certain of the scribes sitting there, and reasoning in their hearts, 'Why doth this man thus speak blasphemies? Who can forgive sins but God only?' And immediately when Jesus *perceived in his Spirit* that they so reasoned within themselves, he said unto them, 'Why reason ye these things in your hearts?'" (Mark 2:5-81,*emphasis mine*)

While the scribes were questioning the acts of Jesus, silently within themselves, the mind and knowledge of God was revealed in the mind of Christ. There was no handwriting on the wall or any angel whispering in his ear. His mind just knew. He had a supernatural knowledge.

This is a much coveted gift among believers but not one that should be exploited. "Mind readers" do exist despite the doubts of some people. Satan has a number of them posing as preachers of righteousness who use their talent to convince the audience that they are of God. This gift, as all the others, is for the purpose of meeting the people's needs at hand and doing the works of Jesus, not exploiting them.

There are troubled and perplexed people who sometimes have problems that bother them but they don't know what it is. The word of knowledge can reveal it. Perhaps ignorantly there are those who have spots in their lives that hinder their relationship with God but they are unaware of these spots and are enlightened through a child of God who is used of the Spirit with a word of knowledge. Again, maybe you are about to make a certain decision in life that will not be good for you. You would make that decision and be heartbroken somewhere down the road were it not for God revealing it to you by the word of knowledge, either working through you or someone else.

Before we go any further, an explanation must be inserted because I know by this time you have this question growing in your mind: "How do these gifts work?"

Notice, that the scripture in 1 Corinthians 12 gives you the number of gifts operated by the Spirit but states "there are diversities of operations." There are so many ways that these gifts can operate that I would not want to be guilty of placing an inhibitor on the working of the Holy Ghost by giving you certain operations.

However, there is a certain feeling that one has when the Spirit begins to move within him. Paul refers to this like having a certain sound (see 1 Cor. 14:7). We sometimes use the expression, "a certain ring." While difficult to explain, it nevertheless is certain when it happens. As with the word of knowledge, no one needs to tell you anything, it's there in your mind just as though you had learned it from a book and you are as certain about it as you know that two plus two equals four. That mental knowledge was placed there by the Spirit. The mind of Christ is functioning within you, the body of Christ.

The diversities of operation in the gift of word of knowledge can come about through numerous avenues. God can reveal things to you through dreams, visions, the written Word, mental impulses through a divine unction of the Spirit, and even through an audible voice. There is no set pattern. But whenever this gift operates, it is for the profit (1 Cor.12:7) of God's kingdom and not personal exploits.

The gift of faith is not to be confused with a measure of faith mentioned in Romans 12:3, which is given to every man. The measure of faith is the "seed faith" that God has given to each of us to cultivate through exercise. It is exercised through hearing the Word and prayer and stepping out on the promises of God. But the gift of faith is a supernatural working of faith that takes over where our faith leaves off. We have witnessed this gift on several occasions in which we were faced with obstacles that were beyond our reach of faith. Suddenly, something would come over us, beyond explanation, and at that moment we seemed to be able to believe God for anything. The assurance was steadfast within us and we had no doubts. That supernatural faith never failed to bring absolute results.

The gift of faith operated through the twelve apostles and the seventy who Christ sent forth in his stead. They didn't go forth in their own faith. Their faith top often failed as was the case in Matthew 17:16, but when they went forth in "his faith and power" they returned saying, "Lord, even the devils are subject unto us through thy name." (Luke 10:17)

The gift of healing is one of the most noted of gifts because Christ manifested that gift so freely. The gifts of healing, of faith and of miracles are sometimes difficult to separate as each requires believing in the promises of God although the gift of faith is above and beyond our faith. The gift of healing is in operation when we are used as an instrument of God to heal. We don't believe that we possess that healing power, but we believe that God does and that he is able to impart the healing virtue through us to the recipient. There is no need here to give scriptural references of the gift of healing as the entire four gospels and the book of Acts are filled with example after example.

The gift of miracles does not necessarily have anything to do with healing, although healing is miraculous. It has been said that anything that God does, if it's done without the help of human intervention, is a miracle. Therefore we can say that all healings of God are miracles, but not all miracles are healings.

When Christ cursed the fig tree in Matthew 21:19 and it immediately withered away, this was a miracle. When it was performed in the presence of the disciples, it made them more aware of Christ's supernatural power.

Mark 6:38-41 is one of the greatest of miracles that is still being repeated today. Christ took five loaves of bread and two fishes and fed 5,000 people and had more left over than when they started. What a miracle! And is God doing the same today? Of course He is. When your bankroll is depleted and your cupboard is bare, turn your eyes heavenward and let the Spirit within talk to God and you will see doors opening that you never knew existed. Just because the figures are not on paper doesn't mean that you don't have the resources at your disposal.

If there are problems in your life that cannot be solved by human means, but are solved, consider it a miracle from God.

The gift of prophecy is so distorted by modern theologians and there's no cause for it. The word "prophecy" means exactly what it says without any extensive interpretation. The Greek, "propheteia" means "prediction." Through the divine utterance of the Spirit, future events can be predicted with absolute certainty. The Old Testament prophets who received the Spirit "by measure" manifested the gift of prophecy in two different ways. Some spoke as the Spirit gave it to them. They were only the oracles of God through which He spoke to the people. Then, at other times, God spoke to them and they related the prophecies to the people in their own words. The gift of prophecy still works the same way today.

This gift does not mean the gift of preaching. There is nothing supernatural about preaching. There are grievous wolves who preach behind the pulpits. Any orator in the country can deceive an audience into believing that he is a preacher.

The gift of prophecy is not preaching prophecy from the Bible. Those prophecies have already been given whether fulfilled or unfulfilled. There have been many who have prepared themselves for future obstacles as a result of the Spirit of prophecy revealing future events to them. Paul teaches that this gift exceeds all others in greatness and necessity. (1 Cor. 14:1)

The gift of discerning spirits is not just a gift of discernment as it has been called. The word "discern" translated from "diakrino" means "judging between" or "knowing the difference between." But the gift is specifically pointed at "spirits." All spirits are not of God. Christ taught us that there would come professors in the last days claiming to be of God and would deceive many; but the Spirit within can discern the difference between the genuine and the fake. It is a much needed gift to operate among Christians today.

Divers kind of tongues is the gift most emphasized among Pentecostal people. We certainly have no intentions of ignoring or discrediting any of the works of the Spirit, but we cannot see things in their proper perspective unless we rightly divide the Word and place things in proper arrangement.

It is a fact that Pentecostals have become hung up on tongues. The gift cannot be discredited but then there is no reason to emphasize it above the other gifts of the Spirit either. First Corinthians 12 does not categorize this as the gift of tongues as has been often stated, but as "divers kinds of tongues."

Remember we have already given you the translated word of "divers" meaning different kinds of tongues. Now, the "divers tongues" are rightly divided into two categories: the known and the unknown. Here, one must absorb the scriptures carefully to understand its full implications.

We already know that Acts 2 was referring to the many languages that were present in Jerusalem on the Day of Pentecost because the scriptures themselves bear this out (see Acts 2:7-8). And yet, the people of Cornelius' household spoke in tongues eight years later but there was no need of different languages here because there were only two different languages present (Aramaic and Italian). However, it was enough to convince the Jews who were with Peter that it was the same outpouring of the Spirit that had fallen upon them at Pentecost. (Acts 10:45-46)

When the twelve disciples of Acts 19 received the Holy Ghost there was no need for different languages and yet "...they spake with tongues and prophesied." (Acts 19:6)

One of the "divers kinds of tongues" is the language of the Holy Ghost himself. This we refer to, and the Bible refers to, as the "unknown tongue." (1 Cor. 14:2) Don't be deceived when people translate this as being "unknown to you but known to someone else who speaks the language." The scripture here alone can show you why this would be a ridiculous translation.

"For he that speaketh in an unknown tongue speaketh not unto men, but unto God: for no man understandeth him; howbeit in the spirit he speaketh mysteries." (1 Cor.14:2) What purpose would it serve for a man to talk to God in a language that he didn't understand? Yet the bible says that "when one speaketh in an unknown tongue that it edifies him." (vs. 4) So, whether he understands it or not, there is something about it that gives him a spiritual lift. A foreign language could not do that, whether he understood it or not.

The unknown tongue is that language of the Holy Spirit himself. When he speaks out of the heart of a man, he is speaking to God. Here is one of the greatest of mysteries. The Holy Ghost within is actually praying for you in a language that not even Satan can understand.

Did you ever feel like praying, but didn't know for what to pray? Were you ever burdened, but didn't know why? Have you ever been troubled, but were not aware of the source? Ah, but listen to the divine explanation in Romans 8:26-27:

"Likewise the Spirit [*Holy Ghost*] also helpeth our infirmities: for we know not what we should pray for as we ought: but the Spirit itself maketh intercession for us with groanings [*his own language*] which cannot be uttered [*or understood*]. And he that searcheth the hearts knoweth what is the mind of the Spirit [*see 1 Cor. 14:2*], because he maketh intercession for the saints according to the will of God."

When once you separate the divers tongues into their rightful place, the rest of 1 Cor. 14 is not so complicated. Much of the remainder of that chapter is dealing with over-zealous people who misused the gift of tongues and were causing more of a problem than good. It had gotten to the place where they felt their entire services were to be made up of tongue worship. This is one of Satan's master tools. If he can't stop a good thing, he'll join you and help you run it into the ground. This is what Pentecostals have done today and it need not be.

Paul admitted that he spoke with tongues and preferred that they all did (1 Cor. 14:5), but revealed that the gift of prophecy was far greater and explained the reasons why.

When a man speaks with tongues, the Spirit is doing either of two things: talking to God (1 Cor. 14:2) or giving special instructions to the saints and this is only practical when the Spirit gives interpretation (see 1 Cor. 14:4, 13).

I like the way Paul concludes this chapter and rarely is it ever quoted: "Wherefore, brethren, covet to prophesy, and forbid not to speak with tongues. Let all things be done decently and in order." (vs. 39-40)

ALL FOR ONE PURPOSE

"But the manifestation of the Spirit is given to every man to profit..." Herein are the purposes of having the Spirit within:

1. To do the works of Jesus.
2. To portray the image of Christ to our generation.

3. To release the power of God to our generation.
4. To reveal the unchanging Christ.
5. To meet the supernatural needs of our generation.
6. To bridge our own gap between the natural and the supernatural.
7. To fulfill our personal needs of the supernatural.
8. To be partakers of his divine nature.
9. To serve him as He would desire.
10. To be witnesses of his resurrection and prove to the world, through the manifestations of the gifts, that He is indeed alive forevermore.

ABOUT THE AUTHOR

Brother Lenard Joe Adkins has been preaching since he was twelve years old. He is an evangelist with God's message for these troublesome days. His ministry of the Word is followed with signs, wonders, miracles, and gifts of the Spirit in operation, as well as salvation for souls and healing for bodies. He preaches on radio, TV, in auditoriums, on street corners, in churches and Gospel tents. He has traveled across America and internationally.

Reverend Adkins holds a doctorate degree and has studied at many bible schools. He has a mission to save the lost at any cost and to help believers to clearly understand the Word of God and all that the Good News holds for them. He is sold out completely to God and is a usable vessel filled with the Spirit to lead others to faith in the Lord Jesus Christ.

He currently resides in Concord, North Carolina.

www.ingramcontent.com/pod-product-compliance
Lightning Source LLC
Chambersburg PA
CBHW052000090426
42741CB00008B/1480